FOURTH
REVISED EDITION

D0001259

A CATECHISM FOR
INQUIRERS

By
REV. JOSEPH I. MALLOY, C.S.P.

Revised by
REV. EDWARD H. PETERS, C.S.P.

PAULIST PRESS ♦ NEW YORK ♦ RAMSEY

Published with ecclesiastical approval.

ISBN: 0-8091-5012-3

Fourth Revised Edition Copyright © 1984 by
The Missionary Society of St. Paul the Apostle
in the State of New York

Copyright © 1927, 1955, 1960, 1965, 1977 by
The Missionary Society of St. Paul the Apostle
in the State of New York

Published by Paulist Press
545 Island Road, Ramsey, N.J. 07446

Printed and bound in the
United States of America

CONTENTS

iii

FOREWORD

When Father Joseph Malloy published the first edition of this *Catechism for Inquirers*, he wrote in the Foreword: "It is hoped that this little book will explain the teachings of the Catholic Church in such a way that the reader may be induced to inquire further into the claims of the Church."

That his hope has been realized is witnessed by the many editions and the millions of copies that have been sold. In presenting a newly revised edition, therefore, the publisher has been careful to retain the original substance of this guide which has served more than one generation as an introductory guide to Catholic faith and practice.

In detail, those familiar with earlier editions will find that except for appropriate references to the Decrees of Vatican Council II and subsequent liturgical changes, the substance of the catechism remains the same, but the order of topics has been somewhat modified so as to stress the plan of redemption as presented in salvation history, beginning with the question of personal identity and human destiny.

This edition owes much of its present structure and editing to Father Edward Peters who was instrumental in preparing the Third Revised Edition.

A Catechism for Inquirers

CHAPTER I

CREATION

1. Who are you?

You are a human, in body related to the beasts, but in spirit a child of God.

2. Who is God?

God is the Supreme Being, creator of the heavens and the earth and all things.

3. What do we mean by creation?

Creation is the act by which God brought the universe into existence out of nothingness.

4. Which are the most excellent of God's creatures?

The most excellent of God's creatures are angels and human beings; hence they are called children of God.

"You have made him [man] little less than the angels, and crowned him with glory and honor" (Ps. 8, 6).

5. In what condition were the angels created?

The angels were, like all creation, good and innocent.

1

6. Did all the angels remain good and innocent?

No; some of them rebelled against God and were banished from the divine presence.

"How are you fallen from heaven, O Lucifer. . . . You said in your heart: I will ascend into heaven, I will exalt my throne above the stars of God. . . . I will be like the Most High" (Is. 14, 12-14).

7. How does God use the good angels?

(a) Angels minister before the throne of God.

"I beheld, and I heard a voice of many angels round the throne" (Rv. 5, 11).

(b) They have been sent as ministers from God to the human race.

(c) They are appointed as guardians over each individual.

"Do not despise one of these little ones; for I tell you, their angels in heaven always behold the face of my Father in heaven" (Mt. 18, 10).

8. How do the fallen angels act toward God and human beings?

The fallen angels, or devils, blaspheme God and strive to draw men and women away from serving God.

"Your adversary the devil, as a roaring lion, goes about seeking to devour. Resist him, steadfast in the faith" (1 Pt. 5, 8-9).

9. Why did God make us?

God made us to know him, love him, and serve him, cooperating with him in this life, and to be joyfully united with him hereafter.

"We learn the meaning of our earthly life through our faith, while we perform with hope in the future the work committed to us in this world by the Father, and thus work out our salvation" (Vatican Council II, Constitution on the Church, § 48b).

2

10. Do we, then, have any obligations to God?

Yes; we must worship God as our Creator and fulfill the purpose God has in creating us.

11. Do we have any obligations to ourselves?

Our first obligation is to achieve salvation; that is the purpose of our existence upon this earth.

> "For what does it profit a man, if he gain the whole world, but suffer the loss of his own soul?" (Mt. 16, 26).

12. What must we do to achieve salvation?

To achieve salvation we must do God's will; that is, we must keep the commandments of God.

> "If you love me, keep my commandments" (Jn. 14, 15).
> " 'Thou shalt love the Lord thy God with thy whole heart, and with thy whole soul, and with thy whole mind.' This is the greatest and the first commandment. And the second is like it, 'Thou shalt love thy neighbor as thyself' " (Mt. 22, 37–39).

13. Is it not mercenary to serve God in hope of a reward?

No, rather it is an act of humility on the part of a Christian to accept God's promised gift rather than assert independence.

CHAPTER II

REVELATION

1. How can we know God?

We can know God by considering ourselves and the world in which we live, because:

(a) everything that there is in the world must have been put there by someone in the beginning;

(b) the orderly development and harmony in the world show that there is an intelligent power directing things;

(c) this Supreme Being reveals himself to us in nature, in history, and in the Bible.

"The heavens declare the glory of God, and the vault of the sky shows his handiwork" (Ps. 19, 1).

2. What is the Bible?

The Bible, or the Holy Scriptures, is a collection of books all written under the inspiration of God.

"For not by will of man was prophecy brought at any time; but holy men of God spoke as they were moved by the Holy Spirit" (2 Pt. 1, 21).

3. How is the Bible divided?

The Bible is divided into two parts:

(a) First, "the books of the Old Testament describe the history of salvation, by which the coming of Christ into the world was slowly prepared" (Vatican Council II, Constitution on the Church, § 55).

(b) Second, the New Testament contains an account of the work and teachings of Christ and of the early Church.

The whole Bible contains 73 books, composed by at least 50 writers, in three languages: Hebrew, Aramaic and Greek, during a period of about 1,500 years, i.e., from Moses to St. John.

4

4. What are the parts of the New Testament?

(a) The four *Gospels*, according to St. Matthew, St. Mark, St. Luke and St. John, giving the life of Jesus Christ.

(b) The *Acts of the Apostles* by St. Luke, giving the history of the apostles after the ascension of Christ into heaven.

(c) Twenty-one *Epistles*, or letters, of St. Paul, St. James, St. Peter, St. John, and St. Jude.

(d) The *Apocalypse*, or *Revelation*, by St. John.

5. Aren't there different versions of the Bible?

Yes, there are many different translations of the Bible, but there is much more agreement than some might expect, especially among modern translations. The Hebrew Bible, of course, contains only the Old Testament.

6. How did some of the differences arise?

Some of the differences arose because early Christians used a Greek translation of the Old Testament. This translation differed from the Hebrew in the names of some of the books, spelled other names differently, numbered psalms differently, and included several books not found in the Hebrew: Tobit, Judith, Wisdom, Sirach (Ecclesiasticus), Baruch, 1 and 2 Maccabees, and parts of Esther and Daniel. Some editions of the Bible list these separately under the heading "Apocrypha."

HEBREW	GREEK
1, 2 Samuel	1, 2 Kings
1, 2 Kings	3, 4 Kings
1, 2 Chronicles	1, 2 Paralipomenon
Song of Songs	Canticle of Canticles
Isaiah	Isaias
Jeremiah	Jeremias
Hosea	Osee
Obadiah	Abdias
Zephariah	Sophonias
Jonah	Jonas

7. How is the special revelation of God conveyed to us?

"The apostles, handing on what they themselves had received ... handed on ... everything which contributes to the holiness of life and increase in faith of the people of God" (Vatican Council II, Constitution on Divine Revelation, § 8).

8. How do we know which books belong in the Bible?

"Through the same tradition the Church's full canon of the sacred books is known, and the sacred writings themselves are more profoundly understood" (Vatican Council II, Constitution on Divine Revelation, § 8).

9. How should we regard the Bible?

The Bible is a record, hallowed by centuries, which gives the history of the Jewish people and the life and work of Jesus Christ and his immediate followers. It was written in three languages—Hebrew, Aramaic, and Greek—during a period of about 1,500 years. Parts are obscure and need a living teacher.

"Philip, running up, heard him [the Ethiopian] reading the prophet Isaiah, and he said, 'Do you understand what you are reading?' But he said, 'How can I, unless someone show me?' " (Acts 8, 30-31).

10. Where is this living teacher to be found?

"Sacred tradition and Sacred Scripture form one sacred deposit of the word of God. ... The task of authentically interpreting the word of God, whether written or handed on, has been entrusted exclusively to the living teaching office of the Church" (Vatican Council II, Constitution on Divine Revelation, § 10).

CHAPTER III

SIN AND ITS CONSEQUENCES

(1) ORIGINAL SIN

1. What names does the Bible give the first humans?

They are called Adam ("man" in Hebrew) and Eve (resembling the Hebrew word for "life").

"The man called his wife Eve because she became the mother of all the living" (Gn. 3, 20).

2. What was their original condition?

Their original condition was one of innocence and familiar association with God.

"God blessed them, saying: Be fertile and multiply. Fill the earth and subdue it.... God looked at everything he had made, and he found it very good" (Gn. 1, 28. 31).

3. How did the human race lose this intimacy with God?

Tempted by the devil, they disobeyed God's command. The Bible speaks of it as "eating the forbidden fruit" (Gn. 2, 16-17).

4. What was the effect of their sin?

This original sin forfeited God's friendship. They were expelled from Paradise, inclined to evil, and doomed to suffering and death.

"Cursed be the ground because of you.... By the sweat of your face you shall get bread to eat until you return to the ground from which you were taken; for you are dirt, and to dirt you shall return" (Gn. 3, 17. 19).

5. Did God abandon the human race after original sin?

No. "God the Father did not leave to themselves the men fallen in Adam, but ceaselessly offered helps to salvation, for the sake of Christ the Redeemer" (Vatican Council II, Constitution on the Church, § 2).

6. What must humankind suffer because of the sin of Adam?

Because Adam represented the whole human race, we come into the world without the special friendship of God; our nature is inclined to evil, our will is weakened, and our understanding is darkened. This is called the state of original sin.

7. Was anyone ever preserved from original sin?

Yes. The mother of Jesus Christ the Redeemer, in anticipation of his merits, was given God's special friendship from the first moment of her existence. This privilege is called her immaculate conception.

8. How can we be freed from original sin?

We are freed from original sin by the sacrament of baptism.

9. Did our Savior's mother enjoy other privileges?

Yes, among them this, that just as she received before birth the grace we receive in baptism, so also at her death she received the redemption of her body as well as her soul, which is the destiny of all the faithful. This privilege is called her assumption into heaven.

(2) ACTUAL SIN

1. Is all sin original sin?

No, there is also actual sin, sin which we do not inherit but commit ourselves.

2. Are all actual sins equal?

No, some sins are serious offenses against God, and these are called mortal sins; other sins are less serious offenses against God, and these are called venial sins.

3. What sins are mortal?

Mortal sin is any thought, word, action or omission (1) in itself seriously contrary to the Law of God, (2) if we know the seriousness of the sin, and (3) willfully and deliberately consent to it.

4. Why is such a sin called mortal?

Mortal means deadly. These sins are called mortal because they kill the life of grace within us.

"The wages of sin is death" (Rom. 6, 23).

5. Give some examples of mortal sins.

Willful murder, adultery, the theft of a considerable sum of money, lies that do serious injury to others.

6. Why should we avoid mortal sin?

We should avoid mortal sin because by such sin we turn away from God and reject his friendship; and if we die in the state of mortal sin, we shall suffer his loss forever.

"But your iniquities have divided between you and your God: and your sins have hid his face from you that he should not hear" (Is. 59, 2).
"The path of sinners is smooth stones that end in the depths of the nether world" (Sir. 21, 10).

7. What is venial sin?

Venial sin is an offense against God which does not, however, deprive us of his friendship.

"Venial" is from the Latin word *venialis,* meaning "easily pardonable."

8. Give some examples of venial sins.

Impatience, uncharitableness, lies that have no serious results for anyone.

9. Why should we avoid venial sins?

We should avoid venial sins because they offend God at least slightly; they lessen our love for God; they weaken our power to avoid grave sins.

"He who wastes the little he has will be stripped bare" (Sir. 19, 1).
"He who is unjust in a very little thing is unjust also in much" (Lk. 16,10).

10. What is meant by temptation?

Temptation is anything that may lead us to commit sin.

11. Whence do temptations arise?

Temptations may arise:
(a) from our own evil inclinations;
(b) from the people with whom we come in contact and the circumstances in which we live;
(c) from the evil spirit.

"For the flesh lusts against the spirit, and the spirit against the flesh; for these are opposed to each other" (Gal. 5, 17).
"Be not emulous of evil men, and desire not to be with them" (Prv. 24, 1).
"And the Lord said, 'Simon, Simon, behold, Satan has desired to have you, that he may sift you as wheat. But I have prayed for thee, that thy faith may not fail" (Lk. 22, 31–32).

12. What are the chief sources of sin?

They are the seven capital sins: pride, covetousness, lust, anger, gluttony, envy and sloth.

13. What should we do when we are tempted?

We should pray to God for help to overcome the temptation; we should strive to remove the cause of the temptation.

"God is faithful and will not permit you to be tempted beyond your strength" (1 Cor. 10, 13).
"He who loves danger will perish in it" (Sir. 3, 25).

CHAPTER IV

THE REDEEMER

1. How are we saved from the effects of Adam's sin and of our own sins?

By the sacrifice of the life of Jesus Christ, our Lord and Savior, who is the redeemer of humankind.

2. Why was a divine redeemer necessary to atone for humanity's sins?

Because human beings could never of themselves atone for an offense against an infinite God.

3. How did Jesus Christ atone for our sins?

Jesus Christ atoned for our sins by his life, sufferings, and death.

"For there is one God, and one mediator between God and men, himself man, Christ Jesus, who gave himself a ransom for all" (1 Tm. 2, 5–6).

4. Why did Christ offer himself to suffer and die?

Because of the greatness of his love for us, and in order to show us how to bear the sufferings and trials of this life, and how to love God and our fellow humans.

"I live in the faith of the Son of God, who loved me and gave himself up for me" (Gal. 2, 20).
"Christ also has suffered for you, leaving you an example that you may follow in his steps" (I Pt. 2, 21).

5. What are the effects of the redemption?

Divine justice was satisfied and complete atonement made for the sins of the human race.

Christ "was delivered up for our sins, and rose again for our justification" (Rom. 4, 25).

6. Since Christ made complete atonement, why are not all saved?

Because it is necessary that we do our part by faith, by keeping the commandments and by leading a good life.

"Not everyone who says to me, 'Lord, Lord' shall enter the kingdom of heaven; but he who does the will of my Father in heaven" (Mt. 7, 21).

7. How could those who lived before the time of Christ be saved?

By fulfilling the will of God as revealed in the Old Law of the Jews, and in the conscience of the Gentiles.

"When the Gentiles who have no law do by nature what the Law prescribes, these ... are a law unto themselves. They show the work of the Law written in their hearts. Their conscience bears witness to them" (Rom. 2, 14-15).

8. Who is Jesus Christ?

Jesus Christ is the Son of God, the second person of the Blessed Trinity, truly divine and truly human.

It is customary to bow the head slightly at the name Jesus.

"Therefore God also has exalted him and has bestowed upon him the name that is above every name, so that at the name of Jesus every knee should bend" (Phil. 2, 9-10).

9. What do we call the doctrine that expresses this truth?

It is called the doctrine of the INCARNATION, which means, literally, "coming into flesh," that is, the Son of God took a human nature and united it with his divine nature.

"In the beginning was the Word, and the Word was with God; and the Word was God ... And the Word was made flesh, and dwelt among us" (Jn. 1, 1. 14).

10. Did Jesus Christ have a human mother?

Yes; his mother was the Blessed Virgin Mary.

11. Did Jesus Christ have a human father?

No; he "was conceived by the Holy Spirit, born of the Virgin Mary" (Apostles' Creed).

"And the angel answered and said to her, 'The Holy Spirit shall come upon thee and the power of the Most High shall overshadow thee; and therefore the holy one to be born shall be called the Son of God" (Lk. 1, 35).

12. Who, then was St. Joseph?

St. Joseph was the legal spouse of the Blessed Virgin Mary, but Mary always preserved her virginity. St. Joseph was, therefore, only the foster father or guardian of Jesus Christ. He and Mary always lived as brother and sister.

13. How many persons are there in Jesus Christ?

In Christ there is only one person, a divine person; but in this one person are united two natures; the divine nature of the Son of God, and the human nature of man.

14. Is Jesus Christ truly a man?

Yes, he was truly and completely human. His body was human flesh like our own.

15. Is Jesus Christ truly God?

Yes; Jesus Christ is truly God, because he is the second person of the Blessed Trinity, having the same divine nature as the Father and the Holy Spirit.

16. How do we know that Jesus Christ is truly God?

(a) The prophets foretold that the Messiah to come would be God.

"His name shall be called Emmanuel," that is, "God with us" (Is. 7, 14; Mt. 1, 23).
"God himself will come and will save you" (Is. 35, 4).

(b) The miracles of Christ, especially his own resurrection from the dead, prove his divinity.

"Do you say of him whom the Father has made holy and sent into the world, 'Thou blasphemest,' because I said, 'I am the Son of God'? If I do not perform the works of my Father, do not believe me. But if I do perform them, and if you are not willing to believe me, believe the works, that you may know and believe that the Father is in me and I in the Father" (Jn. 10, 36-38).

(c) Jesus claimed to be God; this claim must be admitted since he was honest and sane.

"I and the Father are one . . . he who sees me sees also the Father" (Jn. 10, 30; 14, 9).
"Again the high priest began to ask him, and said to him, 'Art thou the Christ, the Son of the blessed one?' And Jesus said to him, 'I am.' . . . But the high priest tore his garments and said, 'You have heard the blasphemy. What do you think?' And they all condemned him as liable to death" (Mk. 14, 61-64).

(d) The apostles called him God, and Jesus permitted them to do so.

St. Peter said: "Thou art the Christ, the Son of the living God" (Mt. 16, 16).
St. Thomas: "My Lord and my God!" (Jn. 20, 28).
St. John: "The Word was made flesh, and dwelt among us. And we saw his glory—glory as of the only-begotten of the Father—full of grace and of truth" (Jn. 1, 14).
St. Paul: "From whom [namely, the Israelites] is the Christ according to the flesh, who is, over all things, God blessed forever, amen" (Rom. 9, 5).
"Christ Jesus, who though he was by nature God, did not consider being equal to God a thing to be clung to" (Phil. 2, 5-6).

17. Where do we find the words and deeds of Christ recorded?

In the four gospels, the first books of the New Testament, written by SS. Matthew, Mark, Luke and John.

14

18. Where was Christ born?

In Bethlehem, a little town in Judea near Jerusalem.

19. Where did Christ live during most of his life?

"And he went and settled in a town called Nazareth; that there might be fulfilled what was spoken through the prophets, 'He shall be called a Nazarene' " (Mt. 2, 23).

20. How did Christ carry on his public ministry?

At about the age of thirty, Christ began preaching and working miracles in Palestine, aided by twelve apostles. This public ministry lasted about three years.

21. Where and how did Christ die?

He was betrayed by Judas, one of his apostles, delivered up by the leaders of the Jews to Pontius Pilate, the Roman governor, and condemned to death. He was crucified on Mount Calvary, outside Jerusalem.

22. On what day do we commemorate the death of Christ?

On Good Friday, the second day before Easter Sunday.

23. What happened on Easter Sunday?

Christ rose again from the dead.

"Jesus said to them, 'The Son of Man is to be betrayed into the hands of men, and they will kill him; and on the third day he will rise again' " (Mt. 17, 21-22).
"This Jesus God has raised up, and we all are witnesses of it" (Acts 2, 32).

24. How long did Christ show himself on earth after his resurrection?

Christ for forty days after his resurrection, showed himself many times to his apostles and others, and proved that he was truly risen from the dead.

"To them [namely, the apostles] also he showed himself alive after his passion by many proofs, during the forty days appearing to them and speaking of the kingdom of God" (Acts 1, 3).

Jesus said to the apostles after his resurrection: "See my hands and feet, that it is I myself. Feel me and see; for a spirit does not have flesh and bones, as you see I have" (Lk. 24, 39).

25. After forty days where did Christ go?

After forty days Christ ascended into heaven. We commemorate this event on Ascension Day, forty days after Easter Sunday.

"And when he had said this, he was lifted up before their eyes, and a cloud took him out of their sight" (Acts 1, 9).

CHAPTER V

THE CHURCH OF CHRIST

1. What means did Jesus Christ adopt to spread his teachings?

"To carry out the will of the Father, Christ inaugurated the kingdom of heaven on earth ... the Church, or, in other words, the kingdom of Christ now present in mystery" (Vatican Council II, Constitution on the Church, § 3).

"And Jesus drew near and spoke to them saying, 'All power in heaven and on earth has been given to me. Go, therefore, and make disciples of all nations . . . teaching them to observe all that I have commanded you; and behold, I am with you all days, even unto the consummation of the world' " (Mt. 28, 18-20).

2. What is the nature of the Church?

"The inner nature of the Church is now made known to us in different images ... The Church is a sheepfold whose one and necessary door is Christ (Jn. 10, 1–10) ... The Church is the tillage or field of God (1 Cor. 3, 9) ... The Church has been called the building of God (1 Cor. 3, 9) ... the spotless spouse of the spotless Lamb (Rv. 14, 7; 21, 2. 9; 22, 17)" (Vatican Council II, Constitution on the Church, § 6).

It is also described as the Mystical Body of Christ and as the People of God.

3. Why is the Church called the Mystical Body of Christ?

Because "the life of Christ is poured into the believers who, through the sacraments, are united in a hidden and real way to Christ" (Vatican Council II, Constitution on the Church, § 7).

4. Why is the Church called the People of God?

Because "Christ instituted this new convenant . . . calling together a People made up of Jew and Gentile, making them one, not according to the flesh, but in the Spirit. This was to be the new People of God" (Vatican Council II, Constitution on the Church, § 9).

5. What is the "Communion of Saints"?

By the communion of saints we mean that "some of his disciples are exiles on earth, some having died are being purified, and others are in glory beholding clearly God himself, triune and one as he is; but all in various ways and degrees are in communion in the same charity of God and neighbor and all sing the same hymn of glory to our God" (Vatican Council II, Constitution on the Church, § 49).

6. Whom did Christ make the head of his Church?

Christ made St. Peter the head of his Church.

"And this I say to thee, thou art Peter [or a rock], and upon this rock [Peter] I will build my Church, and the gates of hell shall not prevail against it. And I will give thee the keys of the kingdom of heaven" (Mt. 16, 18-19).

7. What is meant by the "gates of hell"?

By the "gates of hell" is meant the powers of evil, or of error. These can never destroy the Church of Christ.

8. Who is the successor of St. Peter?

The pope, bishop of Rome, is the successor of St. Peter who was the first bishop of Rome.

9. What authority, then, has the pope?

The pope has the same authority as St. Peter had, because he has always been the bishop of Rome as St. Peter was.

10. In what sense is the pope the head of the Church of Christ?

Christ himself is the true Head of the Church; the pope is his vicar and chief representative on earth.

11. Who are the successors of the other apostles?

The successors of the other apostles are the bishops of the Catholic Church.

12. Must the Church of Christ have any qualities or marks by which it may be known?

Yes; the Church of Christ must be one, holy, catholic, and apostolic.

13. What do we mean when we say that the Church must be one?

We mean that its members must be united in faith, in worship, and in government.

> "If a kingdom is divided against itself, that kingdom cannot stand" (Mk. 3, 24).
> "Yet not for these only do I pray, but for those also who through their word [*i.e.*, the apostles'] are to believe in me, that all may be one, even as thou, Father, in me and I in thee; that they also may be one in us" (Jn. 17, 20-21).

14. What do we mean when we say the Church must be holy?

We mean it must teach a holy doctrine in faith and morals because its Founder, Jesus Christ, was holy, and it must enable its members to lead a holy life.

15. What do we mean when we say that the Church must be catholic?

We mean that it must be "universal" in time and place and doctrine; that is, it must embrace all peoples of every nation and in every age, and teach all that God has revealed.

16. What do we mean when we say that the Church must be apostolic?

We mean that it must be the Church that is historically connected with the apostles, and that holds the doctrine and the traditions of the apostles.

17. How is the Catholic Church one?

It is one because all Catholics agree in one belief, all have the same sacrifice and sacraments, and all are united under one Head.

18. How is the Catholic Church holy?

It is holy because it teaches a holy doctrine, because it offers to all its members effective means to acquire personal holiness, and because so many thousands of its members in all ages have, in fact, attained great holiness of life.

19. How is the Church catholic, or universal?

It is catholic, or universal, because it is not restricted to any one nation or race; its mission is to "all nations." It teaches "all that I [Christ] have commanded" the apostles to teach. It will continue to teach "all days, even unto the consummation of the world" (Mt. 28, 20).

20. Is there room in the Church, then, for racism or nationalism?

"There is, therefore, in Christ and in the Church, no inequality on the basis of race or nationality, social condition or sex, because 'there is neither Jew nor Greek; there is neither slave nor freeman; there is neither male nor female. For you are all one in Christ Jesus' " (Gal. 3, 28; cf. Col. 3, 11) (Vatican Council II, Constitution on the Church, § 32).

21. How is the Church apostolic?

It is apostolic because it has maintained the authority and the teachings of the apostles by an unbroken succession of bishops.

This succession can be clearly shown simply as a matter of history.

22. What do we mean by the authority of the Church?

By the authority of the Church we mean the right and the power of the pope and the bishops, as successors of St. Peter and the other apostles, to teach and to govern in the name of Jesus Christ.

"If he refuse to hear even the Church, let him be to thee as the heathen and the publican" (Mt. 18, 17).
St. Paul wrote to Timothy: "I write these things to thee . . . that thou mayest know, if I am delayed, how to conduct thyself in the house of God, which is the Church of the living God, the pillar and mainstay of the truth" (1 Tim. 3, 14-15).

23. Did the apostles claim to teach with authority?

Yes; the New Testament shows clearly the apostles claimed to teach with the authority of God.

24. Give some examples.

SS. Peter and James and the other apostles wrote from the Council of Jerusalem:

"The brethren who are apostles and presbyters send greeting to the brethren of Gentile origin in Antioch and Syria and Cilicia . . . For *the Holy Spirit and we* have decided to lay no further burden upon you but this indispensable one . . ." (Acts 15, 23, 28).
St. Paul wrote to the Galatians: "But even if we or an angel from heaven should preach a gospel to you other than that which we have preached to you, let him be anathema!" that is, accursed (Gal. 1, 8).
St. John in his Second Epistle wrote: "If anyone comes to you and does not bring this doctrine, do not receive him into the house, or say to him, Welcome" (2 Jn. 1, 10).

25. How do we know that the Church today is teaching the doctrines of Christ truly?

We know this because the Church and its head, the pope, are infallible.

26. What do we mean when we say the Church is infallible?

We mean that the Church cannot be mistaken about any of the truths revealed by God in matters of faith and morals, or about any doctrines connected with them.

27. How do we know that the Church is infallible?

We know that the Church is infallible:

(a) Because Christ promised that the gates of hell would never prevail against it (Mt. 16, 18).

(b) He promised that the Holy Spirit would teach his Church all truths and would abide with it forever (Jn. 14, 16-17).

(c) He promised that he, himself, would be with his Church all days even to the end of the world (Mt. 28, 20).

(d) He is the Truth; his teachings are true, and he must preserve these true teachings in the world (Jn. 14, 6; Mt. 22, 16).

With all these guarantees of safety and divine protection and guidance, we are sure the Church of Christ cannot err in giving us the teachings of Christ.

28. When is the Church infallible?

The Church is infallible when she solemnly defines an article of faith or morals through the pope or through a general council, and also when she teaches a doctrine through all the bishops in their respective dioceses, under the headship of the pope.

29. What is a general council?

A general council is an assembly to which the bishops of the whole world are called by the pope, who presides over the meeting either in person or by delegates.

There have been twenty-two general councils since the time of Christ up to 1964, including the Council held by the apostles in Jerusalem and mentioned in the Acts of the Apostles, Chap. XV.

30. When is the pope infallible?

The pope is infallible when he teaches officially ("ex cathedra") *i.e.*, as the supreme head of the Church of Christ, for the whole Church, on some question of faith or morals.

31. How do we know that the pope is infallible?

(a) We know the pope is infallible because he is the foundation stone, as Peter was, of the Church of Christ which is infallible.

(b) If the divinely appointed head of the Church could teach error in expounding the doctrines of Christ, there would be no security for the members of the Church.

(c) We are compelled to believe the teachings of Christ under pain of damnation. We must have a guide to these teachings who is certain of the truth.

> Jesus said to Peter: "I have prayed for thee, that thy faith may not fail; and do thou, when once thou hast turned again, strengthen thy brethen" (Lk. 22, 32).
> "He who believes and is baptized shall be saved, but he who does not believe shall be condemned" (Mk. 16, 16).

32. What is the benefit of infallibility to the members of the Church?

The members of the Church have absolute security that the doctrines they believe are the doctrines of Jesus Christ.

33. Could we have this security without infallibility?

No; the written Word of God, the Bible, does not explain itself; we need a teacher to expound the Scriptures, and this teacher must be infallible, for if the teacher could make a mistake, we could never be certain of the truth about Christ's teachings.

23

34. How are we to find the means of salvation?

"It is through Christ's Catholic Church alone . . . that the fullness of the means of salvation can be obtained" (Vatican Council II, Decree on Ecumenism, § 3).

35. Are we, then, to condemn members of other Churches?

"One cannot charge with the sin of the separation those who at present are born into these Communities" (Vatican Council II, Decree on Ecumenism, § 3).

36. What, then, should be our attitude toward them?

"Catholics must gladly acknowledge and esteem the truly Christian endowments from our common heritage which are to be found among our separated brethren" (Vatican Council II, Decree on Ecumenism, § 4).

37. What effect do these Christian endowments have?

"Many elements of sanctification and of truth may be found outside of its visible structure, which, as gifts belonging to the Church of Christ, are forces impelling toward catholic unity" (Vatican Council II, Constitution on the Church, § 8).

38. Is it against ecumenism to seek to bring our separated brethren into the one Catholic Church?

"The work of preparing and reconciling those individuals who wish for full Catholic communion is of its nature distinct from ecumenical action. But there is no opposition between the two, since both proceed from the marvelous ways of God" (Vatican Council II, Decree on Ecumenism, § 4).

CHAPTER VI

GOD, ONE AND THREE

1. Who is God?

See Chapter I, Question 2.

2. How can we know God?

See Chapter II, Question I.

3. Can there be more than one God?

No, because God is the first and the highest, and cannot have an equal.

> "Hear, O Israel, the Lord is our God, the Lord alone" (Dt. 6, 4).
> "I am God, there is no other; I am God, there is none like me" (Is. 46, 9).

4. Who are the Father, the Son, and the Holy Spirit, so often mentioned in the Bible?

They are three Divine Persons in the one God.

5. How do we know there are three persons in the one God?

Because it has been revealed to us in Holy Scripture which is the word of God. We believe it, therefore, on the authority of God.

> "Go, therefore, and make disciples of all nations, baptizing them in the name of the Father, and of the Son, and of the Holy Spirit" (Mt. 28, 19).
> "But when the Advocate has come, whom I will send you from the Father, the Spirit of truth who proceeds from the Father, he will bear witness concerning me" (Jn. 15, 26).

6. Are the three persons equal?

Yes; the three persons are equal in all things.

7. Is it not a contradiction to say each person is God, and yet there is only one God?

No, because we say the three persons have the same divine nature and substance, and therefore there is but one God.

8. Can we understand how there can be three persons and yet only one God?

No, we cannot fully understand because it is a matter of God's own inner life.

9. Do we recognize mysteries outside of religion?

Yes; we realize there are many mysteries in the natural world around us; electricity, magnetism, many of the processes of life itself are mysteries.

10. Who is God the Father?

God the Father is the first person of the Blessed Trinity, because he receives the divine nature from no one.

"I believe in God, the Father Almighty, Creator of heaven and earth" (Apostles' Creed).

11. Who is God the Son?

God the Son is the second person of the Blessed Trinity, because he receives the divine nature from the Father. He became man in Jesus Christ.

"I believe in Jesus Christ, his only Son our Lord" (Apostles' Creed).

12. Who is the Holy Spirit?

The Holy Spirit is the third person of the Blessed Trinity, who sanctifies us by his presence with us, because he receives the same divine nature from the Father and the Son.

"Or do you not know that your members are the temple of the Holy Spirit, who is in you, whom you have from God?" (1 Cor. 6, 19).

13. Why is the third person of the Blessed Trinity called the Holy Spirit?

The third person of the Blessed Trinity is called the Holy Spirit because he is the author of sanctity, and imparts to our souls the graces of redemption.

We "attribute" the work of creation to God the Father, the work of redemption to God the Son (Jesus Christ), the work of sanctification to God the Holy Spirit.

14. By what other name is the Holy Spirit called in the Gospels?

Our Lord calls him the Advocate, that is, the Comforter.

"But the Advocate, the Holy Spirit, whom the Father will send in my name" (Jn. 26).

15. Did the Holy Spirit ever appear in visible form?

Yes; when Christ was baptized by John the Baptist.

"Heaven was opened, and the Holy Spirit descended upon him in bodily form as a dove" (Lk. 3, 22).

16. On what other occasion did the Holy Spirit appear?

On Pentecost, ten days after the ascension of our Lord, the Holy Spirit came upon the apostles.

"And when the days of Pentecost were drawing to a close, they were all together in one place ... And there appeared to them parted tongues as of fire, which settled upon each of them. And they were all filled with the Holy Spirit" (Acts 2, 1-4).

17. Who sent the Holy Spirit upon the apostles?

Jesus Christ sent the Holy Spirit after he ascended into heaven, as he had promised he would at the Last Supper.

"It is expedient for you that I depart. For if I do not go, the Advocate will not come to you; but if I go, I will send him to you" (Jn. 16, 7).

18. What was the effect of the coming of the Holy Spirit upon the apostles?

(a) They were sanctified and strengthened so that they immediately began fearlessly to preach the doctrines of Christ.

(b) They were given the "gift of tongues" to enable them to preach the Gospel to all nations.

> "And they [the apostles] began to speak in foreign tongues, even as the Holy Spirit prompted them to speak . . . They [the people] were all amazed and marvelled, saying, 'Behold, are not all these that are speaking Galileans? And how have we heard each his own language in which he was born'?" (Acts 2, 4-8).

19. What is meant by "the indwelling of the Holy Trinity"?

Although God is everywhere through his creative power, even in lifeless objects and in sinners, the three divine persons enter into a special relationship with the person endowed with grace, residing as guests within it.

> "If anyone love me, he will keep my word, and my Father will love him, and we will come to him and make our abode with him" (Jn. 14, 23).
> "Do you not know that you are the temple of God and that the Spirit of God dwells in you?" (1 Cor. 3, 16).

20. What are the gifts of the Holy Spirit?

The gifts of the Holy Spirit help us to respond to inspirations of grace; they are wisdom, understanding, counsel, fortitude, knowledge, piety, and fear of the Lord (Is. 11, 2-3).

21. What are the fruits of the Holy Spirit?

Charity, joy, peace, patience, benignity, goodness, longanimity, mildness, faith, modesty, continence, and chastity.

22. Do all faithful Christians share in these gifts and fruits?

Yes. Vatican Council II tells us that "he distributes special graces among the faithful of every rank. . . . Extraordinary gifts are not to be sought after. . . . Judgment as to their genuinity and proper use belongs to those who are appointed leaders in the Church" (Constitution on the Church, § 12).

CHAPTER VII

FUTURE LIFE

1. What will be the result of God's plan of salvation?

The result will be that "the human race as well as the entire world . . . will be perfectly reestablished in Christ" (cf. Eph. 1, 10; Col. 1, 20; 2 Pt. 3, 10-13) (Vatican Council II, Constitution on the Church, § 48).

2. Has not salvation already been achieved?

Not completely. "Joined with Christ in the Church and signed with the Holy Spirit, who is the pledge of our inheritance (Eph. 1, 14), truly we are called, and we are sons of God (cf. 1 Jn. 3, 1), but we have not yet appeared with Christ in glory" (cf. Col. 3, 4) (Vatican Council II, Constitution on the Church, § 48).

3. How are Christ's faithful now situated?

"Until the Lord shall come in his majesty, and all his angels with him (Mt. 25, 31) and, death being destroyed, all things are subject to him (1 Cor. 15, 26-27), some of his disciples are exiles on earth, some having died are being purified, and others are in glory" (Vatican Council II, Constitution on the Church, § 49).

4. What is the proper Christian attitude in this world?

At the same time that we strive to realize the kingdom of God on earth, "strong in faith we look for the 'blessed hope and glorious coming of our Great God and Savior, Jesus Christ' (Tit. 2, 13), 'who will refashion the body of our lowliness, conforming it to the body of his glory'" (Phil. 3, 21) (Vatican Council II, Constitution on the Church, § 48).

5. Will there be a life after death?

There will be a life after the death of the body, for we possess an immortal spirit that can never die.

"Man goes to his lasting home ... and the dust returns to the earth as it once was, and the life breath returns to God who gave it" (Eccl. 12, 5, 7). Jesus Christ promised that he who sacrificed home and family for the kingdom of God would "receive much more in the present time, and in the age to come life everlasting" (Lk. 18, 30).

6. Can our reason help us believe in a life after death?

Yes; our reason tells us virtue must be rewarded and evil punished; that is often not done in this life; therefore there must be a future life.

7. What will happen to our souls immediately after death?

When our souls leave the body at death they will be judged immediately.

"It is appointed unto men to die once and after this comes the judgment" (Heb. 9, 27).

8. What is the judgment called which takes place right after death?

It is called the particular judgment.

9. Where may the soul go after this particular judgment?

To one of three places: heaven, purgatory, or hell.

10. What do we understand by heaven?

(a) Heaven is a place of everlasting happiness.

'Eye has not seen nor ear heard, nor has it entered into the heart of man, what things God has prepared for those who love him" (1 Cor. 2, 9).

(b) In heaven we shall see and possess God.

"Your reward shall be very great" (Gn. 15, 1).
"We see now through a mirror in an obscure manner, but then face to face ... then I shall know even as I have been known" (1 Cor. 13, 12).

11. What is purgatory?

Purgatory is the state of those who have died guilty of slight sins, or who have not entirely atoned for grave sins, though these have been forgiven. In purgatory they are detained for a time and purified of sin.

"There shall not enter into it [heaven] anything defiled" (Rv. 21, 27).
"Amen I say to thee, thou will not come out from it until thou has paid the last penny" (Mt. 5, 26).

12. Does our reason help us to believe in purgatory?

Since we are convinced that there is a future life, our reason demands purgatory. Most people are neither great saints nor great sinners; they are not prepared at death to enter heaven immediately, nor evil enough to deserve hell.

13. Will those in purgatory go to heaven?

Yes; all those in purgatory will surely go to heaven after they have completely atoned for their sins by suffering.

14. Can we help those in purgatory?

Yes; we can help those in purgatory by our prayers, by indulgences and especially by the sacrifice of the mass.

"Making a gathering, he [Judas Maccabeus] sent twelve thousand drachmas of silver to Jersualem for sacrifice to be offered for the sins of the dead ... It is therefore a holy and wholesome thought to pray for the dead, that they may be loosed from their sins" (2 Mc. 12, 43, 46).

15. What is hell?

Hell is an eternal state of separation from God, and the intense pain and suffering resulting from that separation.

"Depart from me, accursed ones, into the everlasting fire which was prepared for the devil and his angels ... And these will go into everlasting punishment" (Mt. 25, 41, 46).

31

16. Is eternal punishment contrary to our reason?

No. Justice requires that all actions have consequences. The consequence of the complete rejection of God and his love is the complete loss of God and his love.

17. Is eternal punishment contrary to God's mercy?

No. God, in his goodness and mercy, does not force men and women to love him against their will. He allows the choice to accept or reject him freely.

18. Is the existence of hell found in the teaching of Holy Scripture?

It is clearly the teaching of Holy Scripture in many places, both in the Old Testament and the New.

"They shall go out and see the carcasses of the men that have transgressed against me. Their worm shall not die and their fire shall not be quenched" (Is. 66, 24).

"If thy hand is an occasion of sin to thee, cut it off! It is better for thee to enter into life maimed, then, having two hands, to go into hell, into the unquenchable fire" (Mk. 9, 43).

(See also Dn. 12, 2; Lk. 16, 25-26; 2 Thes. 1, 7-9; Jude 1, 6-8. 13; Rv. 14, 11).

Remember, no one goes to hell except by his own choice, as well as by his own fault, deliberately refusing the mercy of God even unto death.

19. Will there be any other judgment besides the particular judgment?

Yes, there will be a general judgment at the end of the world.

"But when the Son of Man shall come in his majesty, and all the angels with him, then he will sit on the throne of his glory; and before him will be gathered all the nations, and he will separate them one from another, as the shepherd separates the sheep from the goats" (Mt. 25, 31-32).

"I saw the dead, the great and the small, standing before the throne, and scrolls were opened. And another scroll was opened, which is the book of life; and the dead were judged out of those things that were written in the scrolls, according to their works" (Rv. 20, 12).

32

20. What is the purpose of the general judgment, since we are judged immediately after death?

(a) The general judgment repeats the results of the particular judgment. Its purpose is to make known the justice of God by showing all creation the happiness of the good and the suffering of the wicked.

(b) In this world the good often suffer, and the wicked prosper. At the general judgment this apparent injustice will be righted in the presence of everyone who ever lived.

> "For all of us must be made manifest before the tribunal of Christ, so that each one may receive what he has won through the body, according to his works, whether good or evil" (2 Cor. 5, 10).

21. Will our bodies share in the joys of heaven or in the sufferings of hell?

Yes, after the general judgment our bodies will share with our spiritual selves in our final state, be it heaven or hell.

> "And the sea gave up the dead that were in it, and death and hell gave up the dead that were in them; and they were judged each one, according to their works" (Rv. 20, 13).
> "I know that my Vindicator lives, and that he will at last stand forth upon the dust whom I myself shall see, and not another—and from my flesh I shall see God" (Jb. 19, 25-26).
> "In a moment, in the twinkling of an eye, at the last trumpet. For the trumpet shall sound, and the dead shall rise incorruptible and we shall be changed. For this corruptible body must put on incorruption, and this mortal body must put on immortality" (1 Cor. 15, 52-53).

CHAPTER VIII

GRACE

1. Can one gain heaven by his own efforts?

No. We need the help of God to be admitted to personal union with him.

"... without me you can do nothing" (Jn. 15, 5).

2. Does God assist those who beg his help?

Yes. He gives supernatural help freely or gratis; for this reason it is called "grace."

"Ask, and it shall be given you" (Mt. 7, 7).

3. Christ died for all; will everyone therefore be saved?

No. Each must prove himself worthy to share in the benefits of redemption.

"Wherefore ... work out your salvation with fear and trembling" (Phil. 2, 12).

4. What is meant by the grace of God?

Grace is a supernatural gift bestowed on us through the merits of Jesus Christ for our salvation.

"We believe that we are saved through the grace of the Lord Jesus" (Acts 15, 11).

5. Are there different kinds of grace?

There are two kinds: actual grace and sanctifying grace.

6. What is actual grace?

Actual grace is any impulse, given by God, which prompts us to avoid what is wrong and do what is right. It enlightens the mind, helping us to see more clearly what he expects us to believe and how he wants us to live. It also strengthens the will, enabling us to conform our actions to his will

"By the grace of God I am what I am, and his grace in me has not been fruitless" (1 Cor. 15, 10).

7. May actual grace come to us in different ways?

Yes. It may come directly by inspiration—the entering in of the Holy Spirit, the Sanctifier. The Holy Spirit breathes life and light also through such means as the example of the life of Christ, through the Sacred Scriptures, the Church, the lives of saintly people, earnest prayer, devout reading; and especially through the sacraments which were instituted by Christ as the chief channels of grace, both actual and sanctifying.

8. What is sanctifying grace?

Sanctifying grace is that which confers on us a new and supernatural state of life by which we share in the life of God himself. It is a prevailing condition, making us his children by adoption, temples of the Holy Spirit, holy and pleasing in his sight; and it also gives a pledge of eternal glory.

"He who abides in me, and I in him, he bears much fruit" (Jn. 15, 5).

9. When does sanctifying grace first enter the soul?

At the time of baptism, for baptism not only releases one from the state of original sin, it also implants the first seeds of the supernatural life. The other sacraments increase or revive this supernatural life.

"Unless a man be born again of water and the Spirit, he cannot enter into the kingdom of God" (Jn. 3, 5).

10. Is it necessary for us to cooperate with the grace of God?

Yes. Without cooperation there can be no spiritual growth or fruit. Anyone who has the use of reason can resist the force of grace.

"Other seeds fell upon rocky ground" (Mt. 13, 5).
"We entreat you not to receive the grace of God in vain" (2 Cor. 6, 1).

11. Can the state of sanctifying grace be lost?

Yes, by mortal sin. It is called "mortal" sin because it destroys the supernatural life within us.

"For the wages of sin is death, but the gift of God is life everlasting" (Rom. 6, 23).

12. How can one regain the state of grace?

By sincere sorrow and the worthy reception of the sacrament of penance.

"Whose sins you shall forgive, they are forgiven them" (Jn. 20, 23).

CHAPTER IX

THE SACRAMENTS

1. What is a sacrament?

A sacrament is an outward sign and effective instrument of God's grace and man's faith.

2. How are the sacraments related to faith?

"They not only presuppose faith, but by words and objects, they also nourish, strengthen, and express it" (Vatican Council II, Constitution on the Sacred Liturgy, § 1).

3. Is the Church a sacrament?

"By her relationship with Christ, the Church is a kind of sacrament of intimate union with God, and of the unity of all mankind, that is, she is a sign and an instrument of such union and unity" (Vatican Council II, Constitution on the Church, § 1).

4. Are there also specific sacraments?

Yes; the Church has been entrusted with special means, vital actions "for carrying on Christ's saving work ... and giving worship to God" (Vatican Council II, Constitution of the Sacred Liturgy, § 59).

5. How many specific sacraments are there?

There are seven sacraments: (1) baptism, (2) confirmation, (3) penance, (4) holy eucharist, (5) holy orders, (6) matrimony, and (7) anointing of the sick.

6. Do the sacraments always give grace?

If they are worthily received in faith and love, the sacraments always give grace, because it is Jesus Christ (through the human ministers) who baptizes, forgives sins, and offers the sacrifice of the mass.

7. How often may one receive the sacraments?

The sacraments may be received many times, except for those sacraments which establish a new relation between the soul and God (baptism, confirmation, and holy orders in its separate grades).

(1) BAPTISM

1. What is baptism?

Baptism is the sacrament of rebirth as a child of God, sanctified by the Holy Spirit, uniting the soul with the death and resurrection of Jesus Christ, cleansing from original and personal sins, and welcoming into the community of the Church.

2. What are the effects of the sacrament of baptism?

By baptism the soul is cleansed from original and personal sins, is welcomed into the community of the Church, is permanently related to God, and joined to the priestly, prophetic, and kingly works of Jesus Christ.

3. Is baptism necessary for salvation?

Baptism, at least of interpretative desire, is necessary for salvation, for Jesus Christ declared: "Unless a man be born again of water and the Spirit he cannot enter the kingdom of God" (John 3, 5).

"He who believes and is baptized shall be saved" (Mk. 16, 16).

38

4. What is baptism of desire?

When it is impossible to receive the baptism of water, one who has an earnest desire to do all that God has ordained for salvation, and has perfect sorrow for sin, receives what is called the baptism of desire.

5. What is baptism of blood?

If one could not be baptized, but willingly suffered death for the faith of Jesus Christ, such a one would receive the baptism of blood.

6. Who can administer the sacrament of baptism?

The priest is the ordinary minister of baptism, but in case of necessity, as in danger of death, anyone, without exception, who has the use of reason, may administer the sacrament of baptism.

7. How is baptism given in case of necessity?

Whoever baptizes should pour plain water on the head of the person to be baptized, and say, *while pouring the water,* "I baptize you in the name of the Father, and of the Son, and of the Holy Spirit" (cf. Mt. 28, 19).

8. Was baptism ever given in any other way?

From the very beginning of Christianity, baptism was given by this method of pouring the water; but during the early centuries, baptism was also given by immersion, *i.e.,* by placing the person to be baptized completely in the water.

9. Why are sponsors required in baptism?

(a) The sponsors or godparents promise what the child is unable to promise for itself; their duty is to watch over the religious education of the child if the parents die, or neglect this duty.

(b) In the baptism of adults, it is usual to have one sponsor of the same sex as the person to be baptized.

Sponsors contract a spiritual relationship with the person baptized; this is a canonical impediment to marriage.

10. Who may act as a sponsor in baptism?

A sponsor should be a practicing Catholic who has attained the age of reason.

11. What should be done if a baptism is doubtfully valid?

The baptism should be repeated conditionally, *i.e.,* with the words: "If you are not baptized, I baptize you in the name of the Father," etc.

12. How are adults received into the Church?

Adult converts prepare for reception into the Church through the Rite of Christian Initiation of Adults (RCIA).

13. What is the RCIA?

The RCIA is an updated version of the way that converts were received into the Church in the early years of Christianity. Through this rite, men and women seeking to become Catholics progress through a series of four stages which gradually prepare them for a life-time commitment to the beliefs and practices of the Church.

14. What are the four stages of the RCIA?

The first stage is the *inquiry,* or instruction in the basic teachings of the Church.

The second stage is the *catechumenate,* which consists of further instruction and formation of actual Christian living.

The third stage is the *election.* It takes place during Lent and is a time of prayer, penance, and quiet recollection for both those who have completed the catechumenate and for the whole community. This stage reaches its climax at the Easter

Vigil when the elected make their profession of faith, are baptized if necessary, receive confirmation, and take part fully in the eucharist.

The fourth stage is the *mystagogia*. It takes place through the post-Easter season and is the time for the new Catholics to deepen their baptismal commitment by sharing the eucharist and by acts of Christian charity and service.

15. Who participates in the RCIA?

The priest, the converts and the entire community of the faithful. Each stage begins with a public liturgy celebrated with the whole parish community. Each catechumen chooses a sponsor to accompany and help him during the catechumenate and the remaining two stages of the RCIA.

16. Who may act as a sponsor for the catechumen?

A sponsor should be a practicing Catholic who has attained the age of reason. Most catechumens choose a sponsor who already knows them and who will be truly supportive during and after their welcome into the Church.

(2) CONFIRMATION

1. What is confirmation?

Confirmation is the sacrament by which a baptized person receives the seal of the Holy Spirit as preparation for the witness of a mature Christian life.

When Peter and John had come, "they prayed for them [the Samaritans], that they might receive the Holy Spirit: for as yet he had not come upon any of them, but they had only been baptized in the name of the Lord Jesus. Then they laid their hands on them and they received the Holy Spirit" (Acts 8, 15–17).

2. What is the effect of this sacrament on those who receive it?

"Strengthened by the power of the Holy Spirit through confirmation, they are assigned to the apostolate by the Lord himself . . . working to make the divine message of salvation known and accepted by all men throughout the world" (Vatican Council II, Decree on the Apostolate of the Laity, § 3).

3. How is confirmation related to baptism?

Confirmation is linked with other sacraments of Christian initiation, baptism and the eucharist. "It is fitting for candidates to renew their baptismal promises just before they are confirmed" (Vatican Council II, Constitution on the Sacred Liturgy, § 71).

"Do you not know that your members are the temple of the Holy Spirit, who is in you, whom you have from God?" (1 Cor. 6, 19).
"Now it is God who is warrant for us and for you in Christ, who has anointed us, who has also stamped us with his seal, and has given us the Spirit as a pledge in our hearts" (2 Cor. 1, 21-22).

4. Who gives the sacrament of confirmation?

A bishop is the ordinary minister of confirmation in the Latin rite, but the priest is empowered to administer confirmation in certain special circumstances.

5. How is confirmation given?

The bishop extends his hands over all to be confirmed and prays that they may receive the Holy Spirit; then he anoints the forehead of each with chrism in the form of a cross. In conclusion the bishop gives a special benediction.

6. How does the bishop anoint those he confirms?

He makes the sign of the cross with holy chrism upon the forehead of each one, saying: "Receive the seal of the Holy Spirit, the gift of the Father."

7. What is holy chrism and what does it signify?

Holy chrism is a mixture of olive oil and balm blessed by a bishop on Holy Thursday. It signifies the strength we receive in the sacrament to combat the enemies of our salvation.

Holy Thursday is the Thursday before Easter.

8. Why does the bishop make the sign of the cross on the forehead in confirming?

(a) Because the grace of this sacrament, like all other graces, comes to us through the merits of the death of Jesus Christ,

(b) To indicate that the one confirmed must be prepared to profess his faith openly in Jesus crucified.

9. What preparation is necessary for receiving confirmation?

(a) One must be in the state of grace and be fully instructed in the principal doctrines of the Catholic faith.

(b) One must select a Christian name different from one's baptismal name; the bishop uses this new name in confirming.

(c) One must arrange for a sponsor as in baptism, if possible the same one. The sponsor must be a practicing Catholic who has been confirmed.

(3) PENANCE

1. What is the sacrament of penance?

It is the sacrament which brings to Christians God's merciful forgiveness for sins committed after baptism, and reconciles them to the Church, wounded by their sins.

2. What is another name for the sacrament of penance?

"Confession" is another name given to this sacrament, though it is only one part of the sacrament of penance.

3. Did Jesus Christ give his Church the power to forgive sins?

Yes; St. Paul writes: "God has reconciled us to himself through Christ, and has given us the ministry of reconciliation" (2 Cor. 15, 18). St. Peter and the other apostles were given the power of "binding and loosing" sins (Mt. 16, 19; 18, 18; Jn. 20, 21-23).

4. Why is it necessary to confess to have sins forgiven?

It is necessary because the forgiving is a judicial pronouncement; it requires evidence which only the penitent can give, if he is able.

5. Do all Catholics go to confession?

All Catholics—pope, bishops, priests, and lay people—go to confession.

6. May a priest reveal sins told to him in confession?

No; a priest is most strictly forbidden to reveal sins told to him in confession. There can never be any possible exception to this rule.

7. What must we do to obtain forgiveness of our sins in the sacrament of penance?

We must do five things: (1) prepare by making an examination of conscience; (2) have sorrow for our sins; (3) resolve never again to commit sins; (4) confess our sins to the priest; (5) perform the penance which the priest assigns.

8. What is a "communal penance" service?

When several penitents assemble at the same time to receive sacramental reconciliation, the service may include Scripture readings, prayers, and a homily. Individuals will then have the opportunity to confess their sins privately to a priest and receive forgiveness. When the confessions are completed, the congregation will reassemble for a hymn and concluding prayers (Ordo Paenitentiae, Caput 11 B).

9. What is the advantage of communal celebration of the sacrament of penance?

Communal penance services emphasize the social as well as the personal consequences of sin, and stress reconciliation to the Church as well as pardon from God.

(A) Preparing for Confession

1. What should we do before going to confession?

(a) We should pray for the light to know our sins and understand why such acts are sinful.

(b) We should make a careful examination of conscience.

2. What is meant by an examination of conscience?

An examination of conscience is an earnest effort to recall to mind all the sins we have committed in thought, word, and deed since our last confession.

3. How can we best make this examination of conscience?

(a) By recalling to mind the commandments of God and the laws of the Church and asking ourselves if we have broken any of them. How many times? And in what particular way?

(b) By recalling to mind the daily obligations of our state in life and asking ourselves if we have failed in them.

4. What must we do after we have recalled to mind the sins we have committed?

We must be sincerely sorry for these sins because they have offended God, and we must make a firm resolution never again to commit sin.

"For the sorrow that is according to God produces repentance that surely tends to salvation" (2 Cor. 7, 10).

"The Lord is close to the brokenhearted; and those who are crushed in spirit he saves" (Ps. 33, 19).

5. What is another name for this sorrow for sin?

Another name is contrition, and the prayer by which we express this sorrow is called an "Act of Contrition."

6. How many kinds of contrition are there?

There are two kinds of contrition: imperfect and perfect.

7. Define imperfect contrition.

Imperfect contrition is sorrow for having sinned against God because we fear the effects of sin—the loss of God and the suffering which accompanies that loss.

8. Define perfect contrition.

Perfect contrition is sorrow for having sinned against God because we love God, and we grieve that we have offended him simply because we love him and know that he loves us.

9. What kind of contrition is necessary in confession?

At least imperfect contrition is necessary in confession, but we should strive to have perfect contrition.

10. When is perfect contrition necessary?

When it is impossible to go to confession, as in sudden danger of death, perfect contrition for our sins will obtain God's pardon for them.

Therefore we should cultivate the habit of having perfect contrition for our sins constantly through life, that we may be prepared for this sudden need.

11. Is contrition for our sins necessary if we wish to be forgiven?

Contrition is necessary for the forgiveness of our sins. Sin is an offense against God by which we lose his friendship, and we cannot expect to regain that friendship without sorrow for the offense.

"Unless you repent, you will all perish in the same manner" (Lk. 13, 5).
"Therefore will I judge every man according to his ways, O house of Israel, saith the Lord God. Be converted to do penance for all your iniquities: and iniquity shall not be your ruin. Cast away from you all your transgressions, by which you have transgressed, and make to yourselves a new heart and a new spirit. . . . As I live, saith the Lord God, I desire not the death of the wicked, but that the wicked turn from his way and live" (Ezek. 18, 30-31; 33, 11).

12. What resolutions must we make at the time of confession?

We must make a firm resolution to avoid all mortal sin in the future, and also the near occasions of sin.

"Go thy way, and from now on sin no more" (Jn. 8, 11).
"Behold, thou art cured. Sin no more, lest something worse befall thee" (Jn. 5, 14).

13. What do we mean by the near occasions of sin?

We mean all the persons, places, and things that have led us into sin in the past and may therefore do so again in the future.

"He who loves danger will perish in it" (Sir. 3, 25).

(B) The Manner of Making Confession

1. What is confession?

Confession is the telling of our sins to an authorized priest for the purpose of obtaining forgiveness.

2. Where do priests hear confessions?

Confessions may be heard in church in a booth called a "confessional," or in an informal conference room setting.

3. How does one begin the confession?

The penitent and the priest make the sign of the cross; a text from Scripture may be read. The penitent may recite the first part of the "Confiteor," after which he states the length of time since his or her last confession, and then names the sins.

4. How does one conclude the confession?

When he has finished telling his sins, he should say: "For these sins and all the sins of my past life I am truly sorry."

5. What sins are we bound to confess?

We are bound to confess all our mortal sins, and to tell the number of times we have committed each sin.

6. What is a mortal sin?

A mortal sin is one that knowingly and deliberately violates the moral law in a matter so serious that it breaks our relationship with God our Father.

7. Can all sins be forgiven by the sacrament of penance?

Yes: all sins committed after baptism can be forgiven by this sacrament if we confess them with the necessary sorrow and purpose of amendment.

8. What should we do if we cannot remember the number of our sins?

We should tell the number as closely as possible, saying how often we may have sinned in a week or a month.

9. What must one do who has forgotten to confess a mortal sin?

He simply must tell this sin the next time he goes to confession, stating that he forgot it in the previous confession. That previous confession was worthy and his sins were pardoned.

10. If we are not guilty of any mortal sin, what sins do we confess?

We confess our venial sins and imperfections, especially any habitual faults. Regular reception of the sacrament of penance provides individualized direction toward spiritual growth, eliminating evil habits, and working for perfection. It is advisable to mention some mortal sin of our past life even though already confessed.

11. Can there be a sacrament of penance without confession?

Yes; If a person is physically unable to confess his sins, he may simply give some sign of sorrow, and the priest will pronounce the absolution, the formula of forgiveness.

12. What follows the completion of the confession?

The priest may give the penitent counsel to help him renew his life. Finally, the priest imposes an act of satisfaction, a "penance," of prayer or self-denial, or of service of neighbor to help satisfy for the temporal punishment due for our sins. Then the priest pronounces the formula of absolution.

13. What is the formula of absolution for forgiveness of sins?

The priest holds his hand over the head of the penitent and recites the formula. The essential words are: "I absolve you from your sins in the name of the Father, and of the Son, and of the Holy Spirit," accompanied by the sign of the cross.

14. What is meant by "temporal punishment"?

It is the temporary separation from God and the pain of purification, as opposed to the eternal suffering of hell from which the sacrament has absolved us. This may occur either in this life or in the next (purgatory). We may be helped by indulgences.

(4) INDULGENCES

1. Must we still suffer for our sins in other ways even after they are forgiven?

Yes; we must atone for our sins even after they are forgiven, either in the next life in purgatory, or by acts of penance in this life.

> "But Zaccheus stood his ground and said to the Lord, 'Look, sir, I am going to give half my property to the poor and if I have cheated anybody I will pay him back four times the amount' " (Lk. 19, 8-9).

2. What is an indulgence?

An indulgence is the Church's special intercession with God for remission of the temporal punishment due to sins, the guilt of which has already been wiped out.

3. How does the Church have the power to grant an indulgence?

"The Church, making use of her power of ministering the redemption of Christ our Lord . . . authoritatively intervenes to dispense to the faithful who are rightly disposed the treasury of satisfactions of Christ and of the saints, for the remission of temporal punishment" (Apostolic Constitution, *Indulgentiarum doctrina,* Jan. 1, 1967, § 8).

4. Is remission of temporal punishment the sole purpose of an indulgence?

"The purpose that the ecclesiastical authority proposes in bestowing an indulgence is not just to help the faithful to expiate the penalties of sin, but also to urge them to carry out works of piety, penance, and charity" (*ibid.*).

5. What are the conditions for gaining an indulgence?

(a) We must be in the state of grace, that is, our sins must be forgiven.

(b) We must say the prayer or do the work to which the indulgence is attached.

(c) We must have the intention of gaining the indulgence.

6. May we gain an indulgence for the benefit of the departed?

"All indulgences, without exception, may now be offered 'by way of suffrage', for the departed" (*ibid.*).

7. What is the difference between a plenary and a partial indulgence?

A plenary indulgence satisfies completely all the temporal punishment due to sin; a partial indulgence satisfies for only part of it.

8. How is a partial indulgence measured?

The measure of a partial indulgence is the fervor and the importance of the good work that is done. The remission of temporal punishment that the faithful acquire by their own action is the measure of the indulgence granted by ecclesiastical authority.

9. How many times a day may we gain an indulgence?

A plenary indulgence may be gained only once each day; partial indulgences may be gained many times each day unless the contrary is explicitly stated (*Enchiridion indulgentiarum*, ⸫ 24 and 28).

10. What are some examples of partial indulgences?

Here are three examples of a general character in which a partial indulgence is granted:

(a) If one of the faithful, doing his duty and bearing the burdens of life, lifts his heart to God with humble trust, adding, if only mentally, a pious invocation.

(b) If he, with a spirit of faith and a merciful heart, puts himself and his goods at the service of his brethren in need.

(c) If he, in a spirit of penitence, spontaneously and with sacrifice deprives himself of some lawful good.

11. What are some particular instances of partial indulgences?

Among the many particular instances to which a partial indulgence is attached are: adoration of the blessed sacrament, pious reading of holy Scripture, the stations of the cross, and the recitation of the holy rosary.

12. Give an example of a plenary indulgence.

The best known plenary indulgence is the jubilee indulgence of the Holy Year, now customarily observed every quarter-century. Because the fervor of the individual is a measure of the pardon obtained, those seeking a plenary indulgence may often be only partly successful.

(5) THE HOLY EUCHARIST
("The Lord's Supper")

1. What is the sacrament of the holy eucharist?

The holy eucharist is the chief sacrament; under the appearance of bread and wine there is present the humanity of Jesus Christ, united with his divine person.

2. Why is the sacrament called the holy eucharist?

Eucharist means "thanksgiving." When our Lord instituted it at the Last Supper, he began by giving thanks to his heavenly Father. The eucharist is the chief means by which we give thanks to God.

3. Is this sacrament also called by other names?

(a) The holy eucharist is also called the "blessed sacrament" because it is the most excellent of the sacraments, since it gives us Jesus Christ himself.

(b) It is called the "sacrament of the altar" because it is consecrated upon an altar and is usually reserved upon an altar.

(c) It is sometimes spoken of as "holy communion," which means the receiving of the holy eucharist, usually in church.

(d) It is called "holy viaticum," a special name for holy communion when received in danger of death.

The Latin word "viaticum" means "provision for a journey." Jesus Christ comes to us in holy communion to be with us on the journey to eternity.

4. What was the occasion of the Last Supper?

On the night before he died, Jesus Christ and his apostles were celebrating the paschal feast of the Jewish law.

"The disciples did as Jesus bade them, and prepared the Passover. Now when evening arrived, he reclined at table with the twelve disciples" (Mt. 26, 19-20).

5. How did Jesus Christ institute the holy eucharist?

"While they were at supper, Jesus took bread, and blessed and broke, and gave it to his disciples, and said, 'Take and eat; this is my body.' And taking a cup, he gave thanks and gave it to them, saying, 'All of you, drink of this; for this is my blood of the new covenant, which is being shed for many unto the forgiveness of sins' " (Mt. 26, 26-28).

6. What happened when Jesus Christ spoke these words?

When Jesus Christ said "This is my body" and "This is my blood," the substance of the bread and wine was changed into the substance of his body and blood. Thus they contained his real presence.

7. What remained of the bread and wine after Jesus Christ's words at the Last Supper?

The "appearances" of bread and wine remained—that is, the form, color, taste, and smell—but the substance of them was changed.

8. What is this change of the bread and wine into the body and blood of Jesus Christ called?

It is called "transubstantiation," which means "change of substance."

9. How do we know that Jesus Christ changed bread and wine into his own body and blood?

(a) His words plainly indicate this; he said, "This *is* my body," not "This represents my body."

(b) Jesus Christ had promised his body and blood as food and drink: "The bread that I will give is my flesh for the life of the world" (Jn. 6, 51). This led to a fierce dispute among his hearers, but Jesus insisted: "Amen, amen, I say to you, unless you eat the flesh of the Son of Man, and drink his blood, you shall not have life in you" (Jn. 6, 53).

(c) The apostles understood that Jesus meant his words literally. St. Paul writes: "The cup of blessing that we bless, is it not the sharing of the blood of Christ? And the bread that we break, is it not the partaking of the body of the Lord?" (1 Cor. 10, 16).

(d) It has always been the belief of the majority of Christians.

10. Why did Jesus Christ institute the holy eucharist?

"He did this in order to perpetuate the sacrifice of the cross throughout the centuries until he should come again" (Vatican Council II, Constitution on the Sacred Liturgy, § 47). The eucharist nourishes the spiritual life of the faithful, helping them to unite their hearts each day more closely to God and to each other.

11. Did Jesus Christ give his apostles the power to change bread and wine into his body and blood?

Yes, he gave them that power when he said, "Do this in remembrance of me" (Lk. 22, 19).

12. How is this power exercised today?

This power given by Jesus Christ at the Last Supper is exercised today by the bishops and priests in the holy sacrifice of the mass.

(6) THE SACRIFICE OF THE MASS

1. What is the mass?

The mass is the sacrifice in which Jesus Christ, through the ministry of priests, perpetuates the sacrifice of the cross by his real presence under the appearances of bread and wine.

2. Is the mass just a memorial ritual?

No; the mass is much more than a mere memorial. Jesus Christ is really present in his risen body, continually offering himself to the Father through the ministry of the priest.

3 What is a religious sacrifice?

It is the external offering of something to God according to a sacred rite in order to acknowledge God's supreme dominion over humankind.

4. Is sacrifice necessary to religion?

Yes; it is necessary to true religion to have a solemn public act by which people acknowledge the dominion of God and their dependence upon him.

5. Were there sacrifices before the coming of Jesus Christ?

There were many sacrifices in the Jewish religion ordained by God, as, for example, the paschal lamb, sacrifice for sin, and sacrifice for reparation. Especially noteworthy is the sacrifice of bread and wine by Melchizedek.

55

"Then Melchizedek, king of Salem (Jerusalem), brought out bread and wine, for he was a priest of the Most High God. He blessed Abram...." (Gen. 14, 18).

Melchizedek and his offering of bread and wine were a special foreshadowing of the sacrifice of the Last Supper, as we read in the Epistle to the Hebrews: "And he, Son (of God) though he was ... became to all who obey him the cause of eternal salvation, called by God a high priest according to the order of Melchizedek" (Heb. 5, 8-10).

6. When was the sacrifice of the mass instituted?

At the Last Supper when our Lord told his apostles to do what he had done, namely, to change bread and wine into his body and blood: "Do this in remembrance of me" (Lk. 22, 19).

7. Why is the mass necessary, since Jesus Christ died once for all our sins?

The mass is not a new sacrifice. By it Jesus Christ enables us to be present as he continues his offering to the Father.

8. How is the mass the same as the sacrifice of the cross?

It is the same high priest who offers and the same victim who is offered, namely, Jesus Christ our Lord. The priest is only the representative of Christ; he does not speak in his own name, but in the name of Jesus Christ: "This is my body ... this is my blood."

9. How does the mass differ from the sacrifice of the cross?

The difference is in the manner in which the sacrifice is offered; on the cross our Lord really suffered and died; in the mass it is the risen body of Christ that is present and is offered, which suffers now no more.

10. What is the office of the priest in the mass?

The priest stands in the place of Christ and speaks the words of Christ at the consecration. It is really Christ himself who is both priest and victim in the sacrifice of the mass.

11. At what part of the mass do the body and blood of Jesus Christ come upon the altar?

At the consecration, when the priest repeats the words of Jesus Christ: "This is my body; this is the cup of my blood."

12. When must Catholics attend mass?

Catholics must attend mass on all Sundays and holydays of obligation, unless they are prevented by some serious reason.

13. What are holydays of obligation?

They are days which commemorate some event in sacred history.

14. How many holydays are there?

In the United States there are six: Christmas, the birth of our Lord (Dec. 25); New Year's, solemnity of Mary, the Mother of God (Jan. 1); the ascension of our Lord into heaven (Thursday, the fortieth day after Easter); the assumption of the Blessed Virgin (Aug. 15); the feast of all saints (Nov. 1); the immaculate conception of the Blessed Virgin (Dec. 8).

15. Who share in the benefits of the mass?

(a) The whole Church, both the living and the dead, gain the general fruits of every mass.

(b) The special fruits of each mass are applied (1) to the priest who celebrates the mass, (2) to the person or persons for whom the priest offers the mass, and (3) to all who are present at the mass.

16. For whom may the priest offer the mass?

The priest may offer the mass for the spiritual and temporal welfare of the living, and for the eternal repose of the dead.

17. Why is a money offering made to priests to say mass?

The offering of money is made in order to provide for the support of the priests. In early times the people gave the things that were necessary for the mass; it is more convenient now to give money, though this must not in any way be considered the *price* of the mass.

> "Do you not know that they who minister in the temple eat what comes from the temple, and that they who serve the altar have their share with the altar? So also the Lord directed that those who preach the gospel should have their living from the gospel" (1 Cor. 9, 13–14).

18. How should we assist at mass?

"Christ's faithful . . . through the good understanding of the rites and prayers should take part in the sacred action conscious of what they are doing, with devotion and full collaboration. . . . By offering the immaculate victim, not only through the hands of the priest, but also with him, they should learn also to offer themselves, through Christ the Mediator" (Vatican Council II, Constitution on the Sacred Liturgy, § 48).

(7) HOLY COMMUNION

1. What is holy communion?

Holy communion is the receiving of Jesus Christ in the sacrament of the holy eucharist.

2. At what service do we receive holy communion?

We receive holy communion usually during mass, though we may receive it at other times, especially in case of sickness.

3. How often should we receive holy communion?

The Church commands us to receive holy communion at least once a year during the Easter time, but she urges us to receive frequently and even daily.

4. What is necessary in order to receive holy communion worthily?

It is necessary to be in the state of grace and to observe the eucharistic fast.

> "Therefore whoever eats this bread or drinks the cup of the Lord unworthily, will be guilty of the body and the blood of the Lord" (1 Cor. 11, 27).

5. What is the eucharistic fast?

Priests and faithful must abstain from food and drink for one hour before holy communion. Water, however, does not break the fast. The sick and aged (not necessarily bedridden) should abstain from food and alcoholic drink before communion for approximately a quarter of an hour; the exact time should not be a cause for scruples.

6. What is meant by the state of grace?

It means being free from any serious sin that would destroy our friendship with God.

7. Is anyone ever allowed to receive communion without being in the state of grace?

No; it would be a grave sin, a sacrilege, for anyone to receive holy communion knowing he was guilty of mortal sin.

8. What must one who knows he is guilty of mortal sin do if he wishes to receive holy communion?

Such a one must go to confession and obtain pardon for his sin before he can receive communion.

9. What are the chief benefits of holy communion?

(a) Union with Jesus Christ whom we really and truly receive.

(b) Many supernatural graces and blessings. e.g., the forgiveness of venial sins, the strength to resist future temptations.

(c) The pledge of everlasting life in heaven.

"He who eats my flesh and drinks my blood, abides in me and I in him (Jn. 6, 57).

"In me is all grace of the way and of the truth; in me is hope of life and of virtue" (Sir. 24, 25).

"He who eats my flesh and drinks my blood has life everlasting and I will raise him up on the last day" (Jn. 6, 55).

10. What should we do after receiving holy communion?

After communion we should spend some time, ten or fifteen minutes, in prayer, adoring and thanking God who has come to dwell within us, and asking for the special favors and blessings that we need.

11. Why do Catholics today frequently receive communion under both the form of bread and the form of wine?

The American bishops recently invited Latin Rite Catholics to receive communion under both forms as Eastern Rite Catholics have always done.

"Communion under both kinds may be granted when the bishops think fit, in cases to be determined by the Apostolic See" (Vatican II, Constitution on the Sacred Liturgy, § 55).

Receiving under both forms is the most complete expression of our sharing in the eucharist. However *either* form is sufficient in receiving communion, since Jesus Christ is really and completely present under the form of bread *and* under the form of wine.

The American bishops, along with those in many other parts of the world, have also approved the option of taking communion in one's hand. This is the way communion was received through most of the Church's history. Catholics in the United States now have the choice of receiving communion either in their hand or on their tongue.

(8) HOLY ORDERS

1. What is the sacrament of holy orders?

Holy Orders is the sacrament through which Jesus Christ bestows on certain members of the Church a permanent charism of the Holy Spirit for special service of the people of God.

2. Why is the sacrament called holy orders?

Because it comprises three steps or grades: deacon, priest, and bishop.

3. Who can receive holy orders?

Any Catholic of the male sex who has the necessary qualifications and is chosen by a bishop.

4. Who can administer the sacrament of holy orders?

Only one who is at least a bishop can validly confer holy orders.

5. Which are the chief powers of a deacon?

The chief powers of a deacon are: to administer baptism solemnly, to distribute holy communion, to assist at and bless marriages, to instruct and exhort the people, and to officiate at the funeral and burial services (Vatican Council II, Constitution of the Church, § 29).

6. Which are the chief powers of a priest?

The chief powers of a priest, in addition to those of a deacon, are "to preach the gospel and shepherd the faithful, to celebrate divine worship ... most of all in the eucharistic liturgy. ... For the penitent or ailing among the faithful, priests exercise fully the ministry of reconciliation and alleviation" by means of the sacraments of penance and anointing of the sick (Vatican Council II, Constitution on the Church, § 28).

7. Which are the chief powers of the bishop?

In addition to the powers of deacons and priests, bishops are marked with the fullness of the sacrament of orders. . . . They are the original ministers of the sacrament of confirmation, dispensers of sacred orders, and moderators of penitential discipline. . . . Bishops govern the particular churches entrusted to them as the vicars and ambassadors of Christ" (Vatican Council II, Constitution on the Church, § 26 and 27).

8. Did Christ give these powers to his apostles?

Yes, Christ gave these powers to his apostles:

(a) At the Last Supper, when he said: "This is my body, which is being given for you; do this in remembrance of me" (Lk. 22, 19).

(b) On the day of his resurrection when he said: "As the Father has sent me I also send you. . . . Receive the Holy Spirit; whose sins you shall forgive, they are forgiven them; and whose sins you shall retain, they are retained" (Jn. 20, 21-23).

(c) Before his ascension into heaven, when he said: "All power in heaven and on earth has been given to me. Go, therefore, and make disciples of all nations, baptizing them in the name of the Father, and of the Son, and of the Holy Spirit, teaching them to observe all that I have commanded you; and behold, I am with you all days, even unto the consummation of the world" (Mt. 28, 18-20).

The apostles, therefore, were to consecrate the bread and wine, they were to pardon sin, and they were to teach all that Jesus Christ had taught them.

9. Did the apostles give to others the powers Christ gave to them?

Yes; they gave to St. Paul, St. Barnabas, St. Mark, St. Luke, and to many others the powers they had received from Christ.

"Then, having fasted and prayed and laid their hands upon them [namely, upon Paul and Barnabas], they let them go. So they, sent forth by the Holy Spirit, went to Seleucia and from there sailed to Cyprus. On their arrival at Salamis they began to preach the word of God" (Acts 13, 3-5). St. Paul wrote to Titus: "For this reason I left thee in Crete, that thou shouldst set right anything that is defective and shouldst appoint presbyters in every city, as I myself directed thee to do" (Tit. 1, 5).

10. Why is a priest called "Father"?

Because he continues the work of the apostles who were spiritual fathers of the faithful (1 Jn. 2, 1; 1 Cor. 4, 5).

11. What are some other titles and dignities of the clergy?

(a) Monsignor, an honorary title conferred upon priests.

(b) Bishop, one who has the power to confer confirmation and holy orders, and usually rules a district called a diocese.

(c) Archbishop, one who has the same powers as a bishop, but who usually rules a larger and more important territory called an archdiocese.

(d) Cardinal, a dignity conferred upon bishops or priests, making them princes of the Church.

12. What are the duties of cardinals?

(a) They elect a pope.

(b) They assist and advise the pope in governing the Church.

13. Who is the pope?

The bishop of Rome is the pope—that is, a man elected by the cardinals to be bishop of Rome. Because he holds that office he is the pope, the head of the Catholic Church.

14. Name the present pope.

15. What are permanent deacons?

In recent years the Church has re-established the permanent diaconate. A deacon is ordained by a bishop after a period of formation and education. Permanent deacons can include married men "of more mature age" as well as celibate young men.

16. Are there other ministries within the Church?

The ministries of *lector* and *acolyte* are open to lay Catholics. Lectors publicly proclaim the readings of the mass, except for the gospel. Acolytes assist the priest at the altar during mass. Laypersons may also serve as eucharistic ministers, bringing holy communion to the sick and shut-in, and distributing communion at mass when there is need. Music ministers lead the congregation in the singing of hymns and certain parts of the mass.

(9) MATRIMONY

1. What is the sacrament of matrimony?

Matrimony is the sacrament in virtue of which a Christian man and woman signify and partake of the mystery of that unity and fruitful love which exists between Christ and the Church (Eph. 5, 32). They receive the graces necessary to discharge the duties of their state faithfully until death.

2. Was matrimony always a sacrament?

No; before the coming of Christ into the world, matrimony, a sacred contract, was not a sacrament. Christ the Lord abundantly blessed this multi-faceted love of Christians through the sacrament of matrimony.

3. By whom was matrimony instituted?

God himself is the author of matrimony. In the beginning he declared: "For this reason a man leaves his father and mother, clings to his wife, and the two become one flesh" (Gen. 2, 24).

4. Who are the ministers of the sacrament of matrimony?

The man and the woman, expressing their consent to take each other as husband and wife, are the ministers of the sacrament of matrimony; the clergyman is the official representative of the community.

5. Are the marriages of non-Catholics valid in the eyes of the Catholic Church?

Marriages of baptized persons who are not Catholics, if contracted in a legal manner before minister or magistrate, are regarded as valid sacramental marriages by the Catholic Church. Legal marriages of other persons are considered valid even though not sacramental.

6. What are the benefits of the sacrament of matrimony?

Christian spouses receive a kind of consecration in the dignity and duties of their state. With their parents leading the way by example and family prayer, children and indeed everyone gathered around the family hearth will find a readier path to human maturity, salvation, and holiness (Vatican Council II, Constitution on the Church in the Modern World, § 48).

7. What are the obligations imposed by the sacrament of matrimony?

(a) The husband and wife must live together in mutual love, fidelity, and patience.

"Husbands, love your wives, just as Christ also loved the Church . . . and do not be bitter toward them" (Eph. 5, 25; Col. 3, 10). "Train the younger women to be wise, to love their husbands and their children, to be discreet, chaste, domestic, gentle, obedient to their husbands, so that the word of God be not reviled" (Tit. 2, 4-5).

(b) "They will thoughtfully take into account both their own welfare and that of their children, those already born and those

65

which may be foreseen. For this accounting they will reckon with both the material and the spiritual conditions of the times as well as of their state of life. Finally, they will consult the interests of the family group, of temporal society, and of the Church" (Vatican Council II, Constitution on the Church in the Modern World, § 50).

8. Can a sacramental marriage be broken?

When the marriage contract is properly entered into between baptized persons, and the persons live together as husband and wife, the marriage cannot be broken except by the death of one of the parties.

> Jesus said: "Whoever puts away his wife and marries another commits adultery against her; and if the wife puts away her husband and marries another, she commits adultery" (Mk. 10, 11-12).

9. May a husband and wife separate for a grave reason?

For a sufficiently grave reason a husband and wife may live separately, but neither one may marry again until the death of the other.

10. What preparations should be made for a Catholic wedding?

(a) The intending parties should together attend the "Pre-Cana" Conferences, Engaged Encounter weekends, or whatever marriage preparation program their parish and diocese recommends. (These discuss the financial, psychological, and spiritual adjustments demanded by married life.)

(b) About six months before the intended date, they should consult their parish priest.

(c) They each must obtain a baptismal certificate of recent date (within six months).

(d) They each must answer the questions of the "premarital investigation" form.

(e) They must obtain from parents or friends affidavits certifying their freedom to marry.

11. How does Catholic canon law affect the marriage of Catholics?

There is considerable legislation affecting marriage of Catholics. Failure to observe the rules may be an "impediment" to marriage.

12. What is meant by an "impediment" to marriage?

It is an obstacle to the validity of the lawfulness of a marriage. This obstacle may arise from nature itself, or from the legislation of the Church.

13. Is it possible to be dispensed from the laws of the Church?

There can be no dispensation from laws which arise from nature itself, but for a sufficiently grave reason a dispensation can be granted from Church law.

14. What is an annulment?

An annulment is not a divorce. It is a declaration that, in the eyes of the Catholic Church, no true marriage bond ever existed. Such a declaration does not affect the legitimacy of children born of that marriage, nor the legal or social status of that marriage.

15. For what reasons might an annulment be given?

Some reasons why an annulment might be given are: if the partners never intended to enter a permanent union or intended absolutely never to have any children; if one partner substantially deceived the other in relation to the marriage, or had significant psychological problems to interfere with giving true (sufficiently mature) consent.

(10) ANOINTING OF THE SICK

1. What is the sacrament of the anointing of the sick?

The anointing of the sick is the sacrament for the seriously ill, the infirm and aged; by it the Church commends them to the suffering and glorified Lord, that he may lighten their sufferings and save them.

"Is anyone among you sick? Let him bring the presbyters of the Church, and let them pray over him, anointing him with oil in the name of the Lord. And the prayer of faith will save the sick man, and the Lord will raise him up, and if he be in sins, they shall be forgiven him" (Jas. 5, 14-15).

2. How is this sacrament given?

First the priest prays over the sick person, and then he anoints the forehead and hands with oil made holy by God's blessing.

3. What does the priest say while anointing?

The priest says: "Through this holy anointing, may the Lord in his love and mercy help you with the grace of the Holy Spirit. May the Lord who frees you from sin save you and raise you up."

4. What are the effects of the anointing of the sick?

"This sacrament provides the sick person with the grace of the Holy Spirit by which the whole man is brought to health, trust in God is encouraged, and strength is given to resist the temptations of the evil one and anxiety about death" (Rite of Anointing and Pastoral Care of the Sick, Introduction, § 6).

5. Does this sacrament forgive sins?

"If necessary, the sacrament also provides the sick person with the forgiveness of sins and the completion of Christian penance" (*ibid.*).

6. Does this sacrament restore physical health?

"A return to physical health may even follow the reception of this sacrament" (*ibid.*).

7. Need a person be in immediate danger of death to receive this sacrament?

No. "A prudent or probable judgment about the seriousness of the sickness is sufficient. . . . Old persons may be anointed if they are in weak condition although no dangerous illness is present" (*ibid.*, § 8 and 10).

8. What about those who are about to undergo a surgical operation?

"A sick person should be anointed before surgery whenever a dangerous illness is the reason for the surgery" (*ibid.*, § 11).

9. May the sacrament of anointing be repeated?

"The sacrament may be repeated if the sick person recovers after anointing, or if, during the same illness, the danger becomes more serious" (*ibid.*, § 9).

10. What should be done in case of sudden death?

Send for a priest if the person is a Catholic. "If the priest is doubtful whether the sick person is dead, he may administer the sacrament conditionally" (*ibid.*, § 15).

CHAPTER X

THE COMMANDMENTS OF GOD

1. Which are the principal commandments of God?

The Ten Commandments; namely:

1. I am the Lord thy God, who brought thee out of the land of Egypt, out of the house of bondage. Thou shalt not have strange gods before me. Thou shalt not make to thyself a graven thing, nor the likeness of any thing that is in heaven above, or in the earth beneath, nor of those things that are in the waters under the earth. Thou shalt not adore them, nor serve them.

2. Thou shalt not take the name of the Lord thy God in vain.

3. Remember thou keep holy the Sabbath Day.

4. Honor thy father and thy mother.

5. Thou shalt not kill.

6. Thou shalt not commit adultery.

7. Thou shalt not steal.

8. Thou shalt not bear false witness against thy neighbor.

9. Thou shalt not covet thy neighbor's wife.

10. Thou shalt not covet thy neighbor's goods.

There is a difference between the Catholic and Protestant numbering of the commandments: the Protestant arrangement divides our First Commandment into First and Second, and combines our Ninth and Tenth into their Tenth.

2. Where do we find the Ten Commandments?

In the Book of Exodus (in the Old Testament), chapter 20, verses 1-17.

3. To whom did God give the Ten Commandments?

God gave the Ten Commandments to Moses, who in turn gave them to the Jewish people.

4. Are we obliged to keep all the commandments?

Everyone who wishes to serve God and save his own soul must keep all the commandments of God.

> "If you love me, keep my commandments . . . He who does not love me does not keep my words" (Jn. 14, 15. 24).
> "For whoever keeps the whole law, but offends in one point, has become guilty in all" (Jas. 2, 10).

(1) THE FIRST COMMANDMENT

1. What are we told to do by the First Commandment?

We are commanded to adore God alone.

2. What is forbidden by this commandment?

(a) This commandment forbids us to adore false gods.

(b) This commandment forbids us to give to anyone or anything the adoration and service that belong to God.

(c) This commandment forbids us to adore God by false worship.

3. How would the commandment be broken in these various ways?

(a) By paganism and idolatry, *i.e.,* by worshiping the false gods of the heathens.

(b) By attributing to persons or things powers that belong to God alone; *e.g.,* believing in the power of fortune tellers to reveal the future, or in the power of spiritists to bring back the dead or to bring messages from the dead, or in the power of *charms* to avert evil or to bring "good luck."

(c) By willfully belonging to a religion or a church which we know is not the true Church established by Jesus Christ.

4. Why are we commanded to adore God?

Because God is the creator and ruler of the whole world, and because all we have we received from God.

"The Lord thy God shalt thou worship and him only shalt thou serve" (Mt. 4, 10).

5. How do we show our adoration of God?

By offering him our humble prayers, and especially by the holy sacrifice of the mass.

6. Is the practice of religion necessary, then, for everyone?

It is certainly necessary for everyone, and those who say it is enough to lead a good moral life without practicing religion are failing to keep this First Commandment.

7. Do Catholics break the First Commandment by having crucifixes and statues in their churches?

No; because they do not adore these. God does not forbid the mere making of images, but the adoring of them after they are made: "You shall not bow down before them or worship them" (Ex. 20, 5).

In the same book of the Bible where we find the commandments, we have the record of God commanding the making of the images of two angels: "Make two cherubim of beaten gold for the two ends of the propitiary . . ." *i.e., the ark of the covenant* (Ex. 25, 18).

(2) SECOND TO FOURTH COMMANDMENTS

1. What is the Second Commandment?

"Thou shalt not take the name of the Lord thy God in vain."

2. What is forbidden by this commandment?

It is forbidden to use the name of God in any profane or irreverent way, as by cursing and blasphemy.

3. What is an oath?

An oath is a calling upon God to witness the truth of what we say.

4. What is perjury?

Perjury is a false oath; calling upon God to witness the truth of something we know to be false.

5. What is a vow?

A vow is a solemn promise made in the name of God to do something pleasing to him.

6. What are the things usually promised in a vow?

Men and women who enter religious communities usually promise in the form of a vow to live in chastity, poverty, and obedience.

Persons living in the world should not make a vow of any kind except after careful consideration and with the advice of an experienced priest.

7. What is the Third Commandment?

"Remember thou keep holy the Sabbath Day."

8. Why did God command the Sabbath to be kept holy?

Because he completed the work of creation in six days and rested upon the seventh.

"In six days the Lord made the heavens and the earth, the sea and all that is in them; but on the seventh day he rested. That is why the Lord has blessed the Sabbath day and made it holy" (Ex. 20, 11).

This need not mean six days of twenty-four hours each, but six periods of time of any length.

9. Why do we keep holy the first day of the week instead of the Sabbath, or seventh day?

We do so on the authority of the apostles. We know the apostles selected Sunday instead of the Sabbath to hold their Christian meetings, because Christ rose from the dead on Sunday, and the Holy Spirit came down upon the apostles on Sunday (Pentecost).

"And on the first day of the week, when we had met for the breaking of bread, Paul addressed them" (Acts 20, 7).

10. How are Catholics obliged to keep Sunday holy?

(a) They are obliged to attend the sacrifice of the mass, and
(b) To abstain from unnecessary labor and business.

11. What would excuse from the obligation of attending mass?

(a) Illness, or the duty of attending the sick.
(b) A necessary occupation during the hours of the masses.
(c) Living at a great distance from the church.

12. What kinds of labor are permitted on Sunday?

Such kinds as are absolutely necessary, like railroading, nursing, essential household duties.

13. Besides attending mass and abstaining from work, how are we recommended to spend Sunday?

We are recommended to spend it in a manner becoming the Lord's day: attending an afternoon or evening service in the church, and devoting some time to devout reading and prayer.

14. Are we forbidden all amusements on Sunday?

No; such amusements and relaxations as are innocent in themselves may be indulged in, so long as they do not interfere with our religious obligations.

74

15. What is the Fourth Commandment?

"Honor thy father and thy mother, that thou mayest be long-lived upon the earth."

16. What is ordained by this commandment?

(a) To love and respect our parents, and to obey them in all that is not sinful.

(b) To respect and obey every lawful authority both religious and civil.

"Hear, my son, your father's instruction, and reject not your mother's teaching" (Prv. 1, 8).
"Children, obey your parents in the Lord, for that is right. 'Honor thy father and thy mother'—such is the first commandment with a promise" (Eph. 6, 1-2).
"Let everyone be subject to the higher authorities, for there exists no authority except from God, and those who exist have been appointed by God" (Rom. 13, 1).

(3) FIFTH AND SIXTH COMMANDMENTS

1. What is the Fifth Commandment?

"Thou shalt not kill."

2. What is forbidden by this commandment?

(a) It is forbidden unjustly to take the life of a human being.

(b) It is forbidden to take the life of an unborn child.

(c) Hatred, anger, jealousy, quarreling, excessive drinking are forbidden, because they may lead to killing, or may injure ourselves and others.

"Everyone who hates his brother is a murderer" (1 Jn. 3, 15).
"You have heard that it was said to the ancients, 'Thou shalt not kill', and that whoever shall kill shall be liable to judgment. But I say to you that everyone who is angry with his brother shall be liable to judgment" (Mt. 5, 21-22).

3. When is it permitted to take the life of another?

(a) If lawful authority commands it in punishment for grave crimes.

(b) In a just war.

(c) In self-defense in order to save one's life, or to save the life of another unjustly attacked.

4. Is it permitted to take one's own life?

No; suicide is a grave sin. We have no dominion over our own life.

"For you [Lord] have dominion over life and death" (Wis. 16, 13).

5. What is the Sixth Commandment?

"Thou shalt not commit adultery."

6. What is the sin of adultery?

Adultery is the sin of a married person who is unfaithful to his or her marriage vow.

"But he who commits adultery is a fool; he who would destroy himself does it" (Prv. 6, 32).

7. Does this commandment apply to anyone besides married people?

Yes; it forbids fornication by unmarried persons, and all actions, alone or with others, that are contrary to chastity, decency, and modesty.

"Do not err; neither fornicators, nor idolators, nor adulterers . . . will possess the kingdom of God" (1 Cor. 6, 9-10).
"Now the works of the flesh are manifest, which are immorality, uncleanness, licentiousness, idolatry . . . carousings, and suchlike. And concerning these I warn you, as I have warned you, that they who do such things will not attain the kingdom of God" (Gal. 5, 19-21).

8. Is family limitation forbidden by this commandment?

No, if the married couple have good medical, eugenic, social or economic reasons, and do not follow a method disapproved by the Church. (Cf. address of Pope Pius XII to Italian Catholic Union of Midwives, October 29, 1951.)

9. Do we break this commandment by sins of speech and of sight?

Yes.

(a) Conversations and stories that offend against modesty are forbidden by this commandment.

(b) It is also forbidden to read bad books, or to witness suggestive plays and pictures, or to yield to sinful curiosity of the eyes.

"Blessed are the clean of heart" (Mt. 5, 8).
"But immorality and every uncleanness or covetousness, let it not even be named among you, as becomes saints; or obscenity or foolish talk or scurrility, which are out of place . . ." (Eph. 5, 3-4).

See Ninth Commandment also on this subject of purity.

(4) SEVENTH COMMANDMENT

1. What is the Seventh Commandment?

"Thou shalt not steal."

2. What is forbidden by this commandment?

(a) It is forbidden to take what justly belongs to another.

(b) It is forbidden to destroy or injure the property or possessions of another.

3. Is it ever permitted to take what belongs to another?

In dire necessity it is permitted to take what is necessary to preserve life, if there is no other way to obtain these necessities.

4. How would business people break this commandment?

(a) A merchant who gave false weight or measure, or goods that were spoiled, would break this commandment.

(b) A banker or money lender who demanded a higher rate of interest than was permitted by law would also break it.

5. How would public officials break the Seventh Commandment?

By appropriating or misusing public funds.

6. What is the obligation of employers?

They are obliged to give a just living wage to all who work for them.

7. What is the obligation of employees?

They are obliged to give a just return in time and labor for their salary or wage.

8. What, in general, are all people obliged to do by this commandment?

Everyone is obliged to respect the just rights of others, and to give to everyone what belongs to him.

9. If we have broken this commandment, what are we obliged to do?

We are obliged to give back anything we have taken, and to repair any damage we have caused.

10. If we have received stolen goods what are we obliged to do?

We are obliged to return the goods to the person from whom they were stolen.

11. If we cannot restore to the proper owner money or property justly belonging to him, what must we do?

We must restore to his heirs or relatives, or if this cannot be done, we must devote the stolen money or property to charity.

12. If we have found some articles of value, what are we obliged to do?

We are obliged to try to find the owner and return the articles to him.

"The accomplice of a thief is his own enemy" (Prv. 2, 24).
"Rely not upon deceitful wealth, for it will be no help on the day of wrath" (Sir. 5, 10).
See Tenth Commandment also on this subject.

(5) EIGHTH TO TENTH COMMANDMENTS

1. What is the Eighth Commandment?

"Thou shalt not bear false witness against thy neighbor."

2. What is the meaning of this commandment?

It means that we must not tell lies, especially lies about other people.

3. What is forbidden by this commandment?

It is forbidden to injure another's honor and reputation by calumny or detraction.

4. What is the sin of calumny?

Calumny is the attributing of faults and misdeeds to another of which he is *not* guilty.

5. What is detraction?

Detraction is the telling of the faults and misdeeds of another, thus hurting his reputation.

"Cursed be the gossiper and the double-tongued, for they destroy the peace of many" (Sir. 28, 13).
"Let anything you hear die within you" (Sir. 19, 9).

6. Is it ever permitted to reveal the faults of another?

Yes; for a grave reason, as, for example, in order to prevent an unworthy person gaining a position of responsibility which he does not deserve; or, in order to bring the offender to correction.

7. What are we bound to do if we have injured the character of another unjustly?

We must do everything in our power to restore his good name by correcting the evil report we have spread about him.

8. Does the Eighth Commandment forbid anything else besides these grave sins of calumny and detraction?

Yes; it forbids all unnecessary criticism and faultfinding, all uncharitableness and tale-bearing. It imposes an obligation as far as possible not to listen to the faults of others.

"Delight not in telling lie after lie, for it never results in good" (Sir. 7, 13).
"Admonish them . . . speaking evil of none" (Tit. 3, 1).
"Set barred doors over your mouth . . . balance and weigh your words" (Sir. 28, 24-25).

9. What is the Ninth Commandment?

"Thou shalt not covet thy neighbor's wife."

10. What is forbidden by this commandment?

All sensual, impure thoughts and desires are forbidden; such things are sinful if they are willfully and deliberately kept in one's mind.

"I say to you that anyone who so much as looks with lust at a woman has already committed adultery with her in his heart" (Mt. 5, 28).
"The wicked man's schemes are an abomination to the Lord, but the pure speak what is pleasing to him" (Prv. 15, 26).

11. Are involuntary impure thoughts sinful?

No; but we should strive to banish such thoughts as soon as we realize their nature, and turn our attention to other things.

12. What is the Tenth Commandment?

"Thou shalt not covet thy neighbor's goods."

13. What is forbidden by the Tenth Commandment?

It is forbidden to envy the good fortune of another, and to desire seriously to have what belongs to another.

"Be not vexed at the successful path of the man who does malicious deeds" (Ps. 36, 7).
"Envy not a sinner's fame, for you know not what disaster awaits him" (Sir. 8, 11).

The Ninth and Tenth Commandments repeat the Sixth and Seventh, but refer to thoughts rather than to actions.

CHAPTER XI

THE VIRTUES

1. How should we truly worship and serve God?

By the divine virtues of faith, hope and charity, we worship God by believing in him, by hoping in him, and by loving him with our whole heart.

2. Why are these virtues called divine?

They are called divine because they relate directly to God.

3. What is faith?

The virtue of faith is a gift of God by which we firmly believe without doubting, whatever God has revealed.

"For by grace you have been saved through faith; and that not from yourselves, for it is the gift of God" (Eph. 2, 8).

4. Is faith necessary for salvation?

Yes, for without faith we can neither know nor serve God as we should.

"Without faith it is impossible to please God. For he who comes to God must believe that God exists and is a rewarder to those who seek him" (Heb. 11, 6).
"He who believes and is baptized shall be saved, but he who does not believe shall be condemned" (Mk. 16, 16).

5. Is faith alone sufficient for salvation?

No, for in order to merit eternal life we must not only believe in God, but we must keep his commandments and those of his Church.

"For just as the body without the spirit is dead, so faith also without works is dead" (Jas. 2, 26).

6. Is it wrong to say that it does not matter what faith we profess?

Yes, it is wrong, for if it did not matter what we believe, it would not have been necessary for God to reveal a religion and for Jesus Christ to found a Church to teach his religion.

"The Church of the living God, the pillar and mainstay of the truth" (1 Tm. 3, 15).
"Careful to preserve the unity of the Spirit in the bond of peace . . . one Lord, one faith, one baptism" (Eph. 4, 3-5).

7. What is hope?

Hope is a divine virtue infused by God, by which we trust in God that he will give us eternal life and the means necessary to attain it, if we do what he requires of us.

"For in hope were we saved" (Rom. 8, 24).
"But they that hope in the Lord shall renew their strength. They shall take wings as eagles; they shall run and not be weary; they shall walk and not faint" (Is. 40, 31).

8. What are the principal sins against hope?

The principal sins against hope are despair and presumption.

9. What is despair?

Despair is the total loss of trust in God. It is a sin against the infinite goodness and mercy of God.

"If your sins be as scarlet, they shall be made as white as snow: and if they be red as crimson, they shall be white as wool" (Is. 1, 18).
"For the mountains shall be moved, and the hills shall tremble: but my mercy shall not depart from thee" (Is. 54, 10).

10. What is presumption?

Presumption is counting on God to save our souls, without any effort on our part to do what God requires of us.

"And if the just man scarcely will be saved, where will the impious and the sinner appear?" (1 Pt. 4, 18).

"Work out your salvation with fear and trembling" (Phil. 2, 12).

11. What is charity?

The virtue of charity is a gift of God, by which we love God above all things, and our neighbor as ourselves for God's sake.

"Thou shalt love the Lord thy God with thy whole heart, and with thy whole soul, and with thy whole mind. This is the greatest and the first commandment. And the second is like it, Thou shalt love thy neighbor as thyself" (Mt. 22, 37-39).

"Now the purpose of this charge is charity" (1 Tm. 1, 5).

12. What are the cardinal virtues?

They are the fundamental moral virtues: prudence, justice, temperance and fortitude.

"For she [Wisdom] teaches moderation and prudence, justice and fortitude, and nothing in life is more useful for men than these" (Wis. 8, 7).

13. Why are they called cardinal virtues?

"Cardinal" means "pertaining to a hinge," and as a hinge supports a door and makes it useful, so these virtues support other moral virtues and enable us to practice them.

14. What is the virtue of prudence?

Prudence is the virtue by which we discern, in each particular case, what is to be done or avoided in the service of God.

"How much better to acquire wisdom than gold! To acquire understanding is more desirable than silver" (Prv. 16, 16).

15. What is the virtue of justice?

Justice is the virtue by which we are always disposed to give everyone his due.

"He who pursues justice and kindness will find life and honor" (Prv. 21, 21).

16. What is the virtue of temperance or moderation?

Temperance is the virtue by which we keep within proper bounds and repress all inordinate inclinations and desires.

"Through lack of self-control many have died, but the abstemious man prolongs his life" (Sir. 37, 30).
"But take heed to yourselves, lest your hearts be overburdened with self-indulgence and drunkenness and the cares of this life, and that [last] day come upon you suddenly" (Lk. 21, 34).

17. What is the virtue of fortitude?

Fortitude is the virtue which enables us to endure any hardship or persecution rather than abandon our duty.

"For I reckon that the sufferings of the present time are not worthy to be compared with the glory to come that will be revealed in us" (Rom. 8, 18).

18. Name some other important virtues.

Three other important virtues are humility, zeal and brotherly love.

19. What is humility?

Humility is the virtue by which we recognize our own unworthiness and acknowledge that all good in us comes from God.

"Even so you also, when you have done everything that was commanded you, say, 'We are unprofitable servants; we have done what it was our duty to do' " (Lk. 17, 10).
"But by the grace of God I am what I am, and his grace in me has not been fruitless; in fact I have labored more than any of them, yet not I, but the grace of God with me" (1 Cor. 15, 10).

20. What is zeal?

Zeal is the virtue which manifests itself in ardent desire and earnest efforts to promote the glory of God and to sanctify our own souls and the souls of others.

"He who causes a sinner to be brought back from his misguided way, will save his soul from death, and will cover a multitude of sins" (Jas. 5, 20).

21. What is brotherly love?

Brotherly love is the virtue by which we wish others well, rejoice in their happiness and condole with their sorrows.

We practice this virtue by performing the seven *corporal works of mercy:* to feed the hungry, to give drink to the thirsty, to clothe the naked, to shelter the homeless, to visit the imprisoned, to visit the sick, to bury the dead; and the seven *spiritual works of mercy:* to convert the sinner, to instruct the ignorant, to give advice to the doubtful, to comfort the sorrowful, to bear wrongs patiently, to forgive injuries, to pray for the living and the dead. On the last day Christ will ask us if we have done these things and he will judge us accordingly. (Mt. 25, 34ff).

"Love one another with fraternal charity.... Rejoice with those who rejoice; weep with those who weep" (Rom. 12, 10. 15).
"Let us do good to all men" (Gal. 6, 10).

CHAPTER XII

PRECEPTS OF THE CHURCH

1. By what authority can the Church impose laws and commands upon her members?

By the authority which Christ gave to his Church when he founded it, to command in his name.

"As the Father has sent me, I also send you" (Jn. 20, 21).
"He who hears you, hears me; and he who rejects you, rejects me" (Lk. 10, 16).
"If he refuse to hear even the Church, let him be to thee as the heathen and the publican" (Mt. 18, 17).

2. What are the principal commands and precepts of the Church?

(1) To attend mass on Sundays and holydays of obligation.

(2) To fast and abstain on days appointed.

(3) To receive the sacrament of penance at least once a year.

(4) To receive holy communion during the Easter time.

(5) To contribute to the support of the parish church and school.

(6) To observe the marriage laws of the Church.

3. What is meant by fast and abstinence?

Fasting means eating only one full meal a day; namely, dinner; breakfast and lunch (or supper) must be light repasts.

"Now therefore saith the Lord: Be converted to me with all your heart, in fasting and in weeping and in mourning" (Jl. 2, 12).
"And after fasting forty days and forty nights, he was hungry" (Mt. 4, 2).
"But the days will come—and when the bridegroom shall be taken away from them, then they will fast in those days" (Lk. 5, 35).

4. What is meant by abstaining?

Abstaining means not eating meat.

Regulations for fast and abstinence are given in the Appendix.

5. What is meant by "Easter time"?

In the United States it is the period of time between the first Sunday of Lent and Trinity Sunday; that is, fourteen weeks. All Catholics must receive holy communion at least once during this time. This is called the "Easter duty."

Trinity Sunday is the Sunday after Pentecost.

6. Why are we obliged to support our parish church and school?

Because in the United States churches and parish schools receive little government support, and must be maintained by the people through collections and donations.

"When the whole Israelite community ... brought a contribution to the Lord of the construction of the Meeting Tent, for all its services, and for the sacred vestments" (Ex. 35, 20-21).
"Do you not know that they who minister in the temple eat what comes from the temple, and that they who serve the altar, have their share with the altar? So also the Lord directed that those who preach the gospel should have their living from the gospel" (1 Cor. 9, 13-14).

CHAPTER XIII

SACRAMENTALS

1. What are sacramentals?

Sacramentals are any blessings, ceremonies, or religious articles instituted by the Church for our use, in order to increase our devotion and to aid in our salvation.

Note the difference between sacraments and sacramentals: The sacraments *were instituted by Jesus Christ,* and give grace to our souls *of themselves;* the sacramentals were instituted *by the Church,* and are merely *helps* to us in receiving God's graces, chiefly by reason of the intercession of the Church.

2. What is the effect of the sacramentals?

"By them men are disposed to receive the chief effect of the sacraments, and various occasions in life are rendered holy" (Vatican Council II, Constitution on the Sacred Liturgy, § 60).

3. Name some of the sacramentals.

(a) The consecration and dedication of churches.

(b) The blessing pronounced on men and women who enter a religious brotherhood or sisterhood.

(c) The blessing given in the nuptial mass to the bride; the blessing given to a mother after childbirth, called "churching."

(d) The sign of the cross.

(e) Various blessed articles like rosaries, scapulars, medals, candles, palms, ashes, holy water, holy oils, incense.

4. What is the sign of the cross?

It is an outward manifestation of our belief in the two great truths of Christianity: the Trinity and the redemption. We mention the three persons of the Trinity, and we make a cross which is the sign of our redemption.

5. How do we make the sign of the cross?

With our right hand we touch in succession the forehead, breast, left and right shoulders, saying meanwhile: "In the name of the Father, and of the Son, and of the Holy Spirit, Amen."

This is called "blessing ourselves."

6. What is a rosary?

A rosary is a chaplet of beads upon which we say certain prayers; the prayers have an added benefit due to the indulgences attached to the beads by the blessing of the Church.

7. What are scapulars?

Scapulars are two small pieces of cloth fastened by two strings or ribbons, and worn across the shoulders under the clothing.

8. Why are they called "scapulars" and what is the benefit of wearing them?

The name comes from the Latin word for "shoulder." Some religious orders, *e.g.,* the Carmelites, have on their garb a long, straight piece of the cloth of the habit hanging from the shoulders down to the feet in front and back, called the scapular. When we wear the small brown scapular (for instance), we affiliate ourselves with the Carmelite order, and share in all their prayers and sacrifices and good works.

There are scapulars of different kinds and colors. To wear any scapular one must receive it first from a priest, and be "enrolled." After being enrolled a blessed scapular medal may be worn or carried instead of wearing the scapulars themselves.

9. Why do we use candles?

Candles symbolize the light of faith. Hence they are used on our altars during mass and other services, and in our homes when the sacraments are administered to the sick, and at the time of death.

10. What do blessed palms commemorate?

They commemorate our Lord's entry into Jerusalem five days before his death, when the people "cut branches from the trees and strewed them on the road" (Mt. 21, 8). The palms are blessed and carried in procession, and some of them are given to the people on Palm Sunday, one week before Easter.

11. Of what do the blessed ashes remind us?

They remind us of death. They are made from the palms of the previous year, and are blessed on Ash Wednesday, the first day of Lent.

12. What is the ceremony of receiving the ashes?

The priest makes the sign of the cross on the forehead of each person with the ashes, and says: "Remember man that thou art dust, and unto dust thou shalt return" (Gn. 3, 19).

13. Why do we use holy water?

Holy water symbolizes spiritual cleansing. The prayers employed by the Church in blessing it indicate its power to protect us from the Evil Spirit; hence we use holy water in blessing ourselves, and the Church sprinkles it upon other religious articles in blessing them.

"Sprinkle them with the water of remission" (Nm. 8, 7).
"Wash me, and I shall be whiter than snow" (Ps. 50, 9).

14. How many kinds of holy oils are used in the Church?

There are three kinds of oils used in the administration of the sacraments:
(a) Oil of Catechumens, used in baptism and holy orders.
(b) Holy Chrism, used in baptism and confirmation.
(c) Oil of the Sick, used in anointing of the sick.

"Catechumen" was the name given to one preparing for baptism in the early history of the Church.

15. When and by whom are these oils blessed?

They are blessed in each cathedral church by a bishop on Holy Thursday (the Thursday before Easter) and then distributed to all the other churches.

16. What is the purpose of incense?

Incense is used in sacred services to symbolize our prayers rising to heaven. God commanded the Jews: "For burning incense you shall make an altar of acacia wood" (Ex. 30, 1).

"Let my prayer come like incense before you" (Ps. 140, 2).
"And another angel came and stood before the altar, having a golden censer; and there was given to him much incense, that he might offer it with the prayers of all the saints upon the golden altar which is before the throne. And with the prayers of the saints there went up before God from the angel's hand the smoke of the incense" (Rv. 8, 3-4).

CHAPTER XIV

PRAYER

1. What is prayer?

Prayer is the raising up of the mind and heart to God to adore him, to thank him, to ask his pardon for our sins, and to beg for his help.

2. How many kinds of prayer are there?

There are two kinds: vocal prayer in which we use a form of words, as in the "Lord's Prayer" and the "Hail Mary"; mental prayer in which the mind and heart are applied to God and holy things without the help of spoken words.

Mental prayer is usually called meditation or contemplation.

3. Are we obliged to adore God?

We are obliged to honor God by adoration and praise because he is the supreme Lord and ruler of the universe.

"I will give thanks to you, O Lord, with all my heart; I will declare all your wondrous deeds" (Ps. 9, 1).
"Seven times a day I praise you" (Ps. 118, 164).

4. What prayers may we say to adore and praise God?

The "Doxology" or "Glory be to the Father" and "Glory be to God" from the mass; the "Te Deum."

5. Are we obliged to thank God?

We are obliged to thank God, because all we have comes to us from him.

"Bless the Lord, O my soul, and forget not all his benefits" (Ps. 102, 2).
"Giving thanks always for all things in the name of our Lord Jesus Christ to God the Father" (Eph. 5, 20).

6. Should we ask for pardon and other favors in prayer?

Yes; Christ himself, in the Lord's Prayer, taught us to ask for "our daily bread," and to pray for the forgiveness of our sins.

7. What is the Lord's Prayer?

It is the prayer Christ our Lord taught his apostles when they asked him to teach them to pray (Lk. 11, 1).

8. Where do we find the text of the Lord's Prayer?

In the Sermon on the Mount, as contained in St. Matthew's gospel (6, 9-13), and also in St. Luke's gospel (11, 2-4).

9. Where do we find the words of the "Hail Mary"?

The first part is from St. Luke's gospel; the second part has been added by the Church.

(a) The words of the angel to Mary: "Hail, full of grace, the Lord is with thee; blessed art thou among women" (Lk. 1, 28).

The words of St. Elizabeth, the mother of St. John the Baptist, to Mary: "Blessed art thou among women, and blessed is the fruit of thy womb" (Lk. 1, 42).

(b) An invocation asking the prayers of the Blessed Virgin, added by the Church: "Holy Mary, Mother of God, pray for us sinners now, and at the hour of our death. Amen."

10. When should we pray?

We should pray frequently, but especially morning and evening, before and after meals, when we are in physical or spiritual danger.

We must "always pray and not lose heart" (Lk. 18, 1).
"Pray without ceasing" (1 Thes. 5, 17.)

94

11. To whom may we pray?

(a) First we must pray to God, Father, Son, and Holy Spirit.

(b) We may pray to the Blessed Virgin, to the angels and saints, in order to ask them in turn to pray for us.

"And with the prayers of the saints there went up before God from the angel's hand the smoke of the incense" (Rv. 8, 4).

12. For whom should we pray?

(a) We should pray for the living, both for ourselves and others whom we desire God to help.

"I urge therefore, first of all, that supplications, prayers, intercessions and thanksgivings be made for all men" (1 Tm. 2, 1).
"Pray for one another, that you may be saved. For the unceasing prayer of a just man is of great avail" (Jas. 5, 16).

(b) We should pray for the dead.

"It is therefore a holy and wholesome thought to pray for the dead, that they may be loosed from their sins" (2 Mc. 12, 46).

13. Why should we pray for the dead?

Because we are united with them in "the communion of saints," and the merits of our good works and prayers reach the dead "who die in the Lord" (Rv. 14, 13), but who have not yet entered heaven.

14. What qualities should our prayers have?

Our prayers should be attentive, humble, confident, and persevering.

"Let us therefore draw near with confidence to the throne of grace" (Heb. 4, 16).
"Know ye that the Lord will hear your prayers, if you continue with perseverance in fastings and prayers in the sight of the Lord" (Jdt. 4, 11).

CHAPTER XV

BLESSED VIRGIN, SAINTS, AND DEVOTIONS

1. Who was the Blessed Virgin Mary?

She was the mother of Christ.

2. Is Mary truly the mother of God?

She is truly the mother of God, because Jesus Christ is the second person of the Blessed Trinity, equal to the Father and the Holy Spirit, and truly God.

"But when the fullness of time came, God sent his Son, born of a woman, born under the Law" (Gal. 4, 4).

3. Does Mary interfere with our devotion to Christ?

"The maternal duty of Mary toward men in no way obscures or diminishes the unique mediation of Christ, but rather shows his power ... It rests on his mediation, depends entirely upon it and draws all its power from it. In no way does it impede, but rather does it foster the immediate union of the faithful with Christ" (Vatican Council II, Constitution on the Church, § 60).

4. What are the principal doctrines of the Church concerning the Blessed Virgin Mary?

(a) Her immaculate conception.
(b) Her perpetual virginity.
(c) Her assumption into heaven.

5. What is meant by the immaculate conception?

The immaculate conception means that the soul of the Blessed Virgin was preserved from original sin from her conception, *i.e.*, from the beginning of her existence.

6. What is meant by the perpetual virginity of Mary?

By the perpetual virginity of Mary is meant that both before and after the birth of Jesus Christ she preserved her virginity.

"Mary said to the angel, 'How shall this happen, since I do not know man?' " (Lk. 1, 34).

7. What do we mean by the assumption of the Blessed Virgin?

When she departed this earth, Mary was "assumed" or taken into heaven, body and soul, and crowned as its Queen.

8. What was the reason for the Blessed Virgin's assumption into heaven?

God wished to preserve her body from the decay that follows death, because from her Jesus Christ took his human nature.

It is the Christian belief that all bodies will rise from the grave at the end of the world; in the case of the Blessed Virgin this was simply anticipated. Her body was not allowed to suffer corruption.

9. When do we commemorate the assumption?

On August 15. In the United States it is a holy day on which Catholics must attend mass.

10. Who are the saints?

The saints are men and women who led lives of great holiness and who are now in heaven.

11. Why do we honor the saints?

Because they were heroes in God's service: the apostles and disciples of Jesus Christ; the martyrs, *i.e.,* those who were put to death for their Catholic faith; the hundreds of devout men and women who lived in great holiness, as active missionaries and in quiet prayer.

12. May we pray to the Blessed Virgin and the saints?

We may pray to the Blessed Virgin and the saints to ask them in turn, to pray for us.

"The twenty-four elders fell down before the Lamb, having . . . golden bowls full of incense, which are the prayers of the saints . . . and with the prayers of the saints there went up before God from the angel's hand the smoke of the incense" (Rv. 5, 8; 8, 4).

Note that we do not expect the Blessed Virgin or the saints to do anything for us by their own power; we merely ask their prayers and intercessions with God.

13. What are relics?

Relics are the remains of some sacred person or thing, as a piece of the Cross upon which Christ died, or a piece of bone from the body of some saint, or of something belonging to a saint.

14. Why do we honor relics?

We honor relics because of their sacred associations; just as we honor the remains of our national heroes, the Liberty Bell, the flags that have been through battle, and the playthings of a dead child.

15. Besides the mass and the sacraments what are some of the chief devotions in the Catholic Church?

(a) Benediction of the Most Blessed Sacrament.
(b) The devotion to the Sacred Heart of Jesus.
(c) The Stations of the Cross.

(d) The Rosary of the Blessed Virgin.

(e) Novenas to our Lord and the saints.

16. What is Benediction of the Most Blessed Sacrament?

Benediction is a blessing with the blessed sacrament, accompanied by hymns and prayers.

17. What is the devotion to the sacred heart of Jesus?

It is the devotion to the sacred heart as the symbol of Christ's great love for us.

The First Friday of each month is dedicated to the sacred heart.

18. What are the Stations of the Cross?

They are fourteen incidents that happened between the trial of Christ by Pilate, and his death and burial; usually they are represented by pictures of these events upon the walls of the church.

19. What is the rosary of the Blessed Virgin?

The rosary is a devotion in which we meditate upon fifteen "mysteries," or events, in the life of Jesus Christ and his Blessed Mother, while we say certain prayers.

20. What are the prayers in the rosary?

The Apostles' Creed, the Lord's Prayer, the Hail Mary, the Glory be to the Father.

21. What are the "mysteries" of the rosary?

(a) The joyful mysteries:

1. The Annunciation; that is, the message brought to Mary by the Angel Gabriel (Lk. 1, 26-28).
2. The Visitation of Mary to her cousin St. Elizabeth (Lk. 1, 39-56).
3. The Birth of Jesus Christ (Lk. 2, 1-20).
4. The Presentation of Jesus in the Temple (Lk. 2, 22-39).
5. The Finding of Jesus in the Temple (Lk. 2, 42-52).

(b) The sorrowful mysteries:

1. The Agony and Prayer of Jesus in the Garden of Gethsemane (Mt. 27, 33-54).
2. The Scourging of Jesus (Mt. 27, 26).
3. The Crowning with Thorns (Mt. 27, 28-31).
4. The Carrying of the Cross (Lk. 23, 26-32).
5. The Crucifixion (Mt. 17, 33-50; Lk. 23, 33-49; Jn. 19, 17-37).

(c) The glorious mysteries:

1. The Resurrection of Jesus (Jn. 20, 1-23).
2. The Ascension into Heaven (Mk. 16, 14-20; Acts 1, 1-12).
3. The Coming of the Holy Spirit (Acts 2, 1-4).
4. The Assumption of the Blessed Virgin into Heaven.
5. The Coronation of the Blessed Virgin Queen of Heaven.

22. What is a novena?

A novena is a period of nine days' prayer in preparation for a festival of the Church.

CHAPTER XVI

CATHOLIC PRAYERS

1. The Sign of the Cross

In the name of the Father, and of the Son, and of the Holy Spirit. Amen.

2. Morning Offering

O Jesus, through the immaculate heart of Mary, I offer thee my prayers, works and sufferings of this day for all the intentions of thy sacred heart, in union with the holy sacrifice of the mass throughout the world.

3. The Lord's Prayer

Our Father, who art in heaven, hallowed be thy name; thy kingdom come; thy will be done on earth as it is in heaven. Give us this day our daily bread; and forgive us our trespasses as we forgive those who trespass against us; and lead us not into temptation, but deliver us from evil. Amen.

4. The Hail Mary

Hail Mary, full of grace! The Lord is with thee; blessed art thou amongst women, and blessed is the fruit of thy womb, Jesus. Holy Mary, mother of God, pray for us sinners now and at the hour of our death. Amen.

5. The Doxology

Glory be to the Father, and to the Son, and to the Holy Spirit, as it was in the beginning, is now, and ever shall be, world without end. Amen.

6. The Apostles' Creed

I believe in God, the Father almighty, creator of heaven and earth; and in Jesus Christ, his only Son, our Lord; who was conceived by the Holy Spirit, born of the Virgin Mary, suffered under Pontius Pilate, was crucified, died, and was buried. He descended into hell; the third day he rose again from the dead; he ascended into heaven, sitteth at the right hand of God, the Father almighty; from thence he shall come to judge the living and the dead. I believe in the Holy Spirit, the holy Catholic Church, the communion of saints, the forgiveness of sins, the resurrection of the body, and life everlasting. Amen.

7. The Confiteor

I confess to almighty God, to blessed Mary, ever virgin, to blessed Michael the archangel, to blessed John the Baptist, to the holy apostles Peter and Paul, and to all the saints, that I have sinned exceedingly in thought, word, and deed, through my fault, through my fault, through my most grievous fault. Therefore, I beseech blessed Mary, ever virgin, blessed Michael the archangel, blessed John the Baptist, the holy apostles Peter and Paul, and all the saints, to pray to the Lord our God for me.

May the almighty God have mercy on me, and forgive me my sins, and bring me to everlasting life. Amen.

May the almighty and merciful Lord grant me pardon, absolution, and remission of all my sins. Amen.

8. A Short Act of Contrition, or Sorrow for Sin

O my God! I am truly sorry for all my sins, because they have offended thee, who art so good and worthy of all my love. I firmly resolve by thy holy grace never again to commit sin.

9. Another Act of Contrition

O my God! I am heartily sorry for having offended thee, and I detest all my sins, because I dread the loss of heaven and the pains of hell, but most of all because they offend thee, my God, who art all-good and deserving of all my love. I firmly resolve, with the help of thy grace, to confess my sins, to do penance, and to amend all my life.

10. An Act of Faith

O my God! I firmly believe that thou art one God in three divine persons, Father, Son, and Holy Spirit; I believe that thy divine Son became man, and died for our sins, and that he will come to judge the living and the dead. I believe these and all the truths which the holy Catholic Church teaches, because thou hast revealed them, who canst neither deceive nor be deceived.

11. An Act of Hope

O my God! Relying on thy infinite goodness and promises, I hope to obtain pardon of my sins, the help of thy grace, and life everlasting, through the merits of Jesus Christ, my Lord and redeemer.

12. An Act of Love

O my God! I love thee above all things, with my whole heart and soul, because thou art all-good and worthy of all love. I love my neighbor as myself for the love of thee. I forgive all who have injured me, and ask pardon of all whom I have injured.

13. An Act of Thanksgiving

O my God! I give thee thanks from the bottom of my heart for the mercies and blessings which thou hast bestowed upon me; above all because thou hast loved me from all eternity and hast sent thy divine Son, our Lord Jesus Christ, to redeem me with his precious blood.

14. The Blessing Before Meals

Bless us, O Lord! and these thy gifts, which we are about to receive from thy bounty, through Christ our Lord. Amen.

15. Grace After Meals

We give thee thanks for all thy benefits, O almighty God, who livest and reignest for ever; and may the souls of the faithful departed, through the mercy of God, rest in peace. Amen.

16. Divine Praises

Blessed be God
Blessed be his holy name
Blessed be Jesus Christ, true God and true man
Blessed be the name of Jesus
Blessed be his most sacred heart
Blessed be his most precious blood
Blessed be Jesus in the most holy sacrament of the altar
Blessed be the Holy Spirit, the Paraclete
Blessed be the great mother of God, Mary most holy
Blessed be her holy and immaculate conception
Blessed be her glorious assumption
Blessed be the name of Mary, virgin and mother
Blessed be Saint Joseph, her most chaste spouse
Blessed be God in his angels and in his saints

APPENDIX

RITE OF RECEPTION
OF A BAPTIZED CHRISTIAN
INTO FULL COMMUNION*

The ceremony takes place, if possible, at mass, or with a hymn, Scripture reading, and homily. Then the priest invites the candidate to come forward with his sponsor, using these or similar words:

"N., you have asked to be received into full communion with the Catholic Church. You have made your decision after careful thought under the guidance of the Holy Spirit. Now come forward with your sponsor and profess the Catholic faith in the presence of this community. This is the faith in which, for the first time, you will be one with us at the eucharistic table of the Lord Jesus, the sign of the Church's unity."

The one to be received then recites the Nicene Creed with the faithful, and adds:

"I believe and profess all the holy Catholic Church teaches, and proclaims to be revealed by God."

In many cases the rite of confirmation follows. If the one received is not given confirmation, the priest says:

"N., the Lord receives you into the Catholic Church. His love has led you here so that, in the unity of the Holy Spirit, you may have full communion with us in the faith that you have professed in the presence of this family."

The general intercessions follow and (if mass is not said) the Lord's Prayer is sung or recited by all present. Then the priest gives his blessing, and the congregation may greet the newly received person in a friendly way. Then all depart in peace.

---

*Cf. Provisional text approved by the Bishops' Committee on the Liturgy, Washington, 1973.

FASTING AND ABSTINENCE

The Apostolic Constitution "Poenitemini" of February 17, 1966 sees "in the traditional trials of 'prayer—fasting—charity' the fundamental means of complying with the divine precepts of penitence." It goes on to give the following details:

"1. The law of abstinence forbids the use of meat, but not of eggs, products of milk, or condiments made of animal fat.

"2. The law of fasting allows one full meal a day, but does not prohibit taking some food in the morning and evening, preserving—as far as quantity and quality are concerned—approved local custom." (Common American custom indicates that the two smaller meals together should not make a full meal.)

The Apostolic Constitution states to whom these laws apply: "To the law of abstinence those are bound who have completed their 14th year of age. To the law of fast those of the faithful are bound who have completed their 21st year and up until the beginning of their 60th year." It notes, however, that pastors "for just cause and in accordance with the prescriptions of the Ordinary may grant to individual faithful as well as individual families dispensation or commutation of abstinence and fast into other pious practices."

A Pastoral Statement of the Bishops of the United States, November 18, 1966, declared that vigils and ember days no longer oblige the faithful to fast and abstinence, and they went on to say: "We hereby terminate the traditional law of abstinence as binding under pain of sin, as the sole prescribed means of observing Friday," but they insisted that "the obligation to fast and to abstain from meat . . . still binds on Ash Wednesday and Good Friday," and they added: "We preserve for our dioceses the tradition of abstinence from meat on each of the Fridays of Lent, confident that no Catholic Christian will lightly excuse himself from this penitential practice."

EUCHARISTIC FAST

Saint Augustine wrote 1,500 years ago that "the most holy Eucharist is always received fasting . . . throughout the world." In 1964 Pope Paul introduced the rule of the one-hour eucharistic fast from solid food and liquids (apart from water). The Congregation for the Sacraments has reduced the eucharistic fast from food and alcoholic drink for the sick and aged to approximately one quarter of an hour and has noted that the exact time should be no cause for scrupulosity or worry.